THE KRUSTY BOOK

HarperCollins*Publishers*

KRUSTY'S
TOP 40

THE KRUSTY BOOK

THE SIMPSONS™ LIBRARY OF WISDOM
THE KRUSTY BOOK

HarperCollins*Publishers*
77–85 Fulham Palace Road
Hammersmith, London W6 8JB
www.harpercollins.co.uk

Published by HarperCollins 2006
1 3 5 7 9 8 6 4 2

ISBN-13 0-00-723453-8
ISBN-10 978-0-00-723453-0

Printed and bound in Italy by L.E.G.O. SpA

Publisher: Matt Groening
Creative Director: Bill Morrison
Managing Editor: Terry Delegeane
Director of Operations: Robert Zaugh
Art Director: Nathan Kane
Special Projects Art Director: Serban Cristescu
Production Manager: Christopher Ungar
Production/Design: Karen Bates, Art Villanueva
Staff Artists: Chia-Hsien Jason Ho, Mike Rote
Production Assistant: Nathan Hamill
Administration: Sherri Smith
Legal Guardian: Susan A. Grode

THE SIMPSONS™ LIBRARY OF WISDOM

Conceived and Edited by Bill Morrison
Book Design and Production by Serban Cristescu
Contributing Editor: Terry Delegeane

Contributing Artists:
KAREN BATES, JOHN COSTANZA, SERBAN CRISTESCU, MIKE DECARLO, FRANCIS DINGLASAN, LUIS ESCOBAR, NATHAN HAMILL, CHIA-HSIEN JASON HO, NATHAN KANE, ISTVAN MAJOROS, JEANETTE MORENO, BILL MORRISON, KEVIN M. NEWMAN, JOEY NILGES, MIKE ROTE, KEVIN SEGNA, CHRIS UNGAR

Contributing Writers:
JAMIE ANGELL, SCOTT M. GIMPLE, JESSE LEON McCANN, BILL MORRISON, TOM PEYER, MARY TRAINOR

Special Thanks to:
Pete Benson, N. Vyolet Diaz, Deanna MacLellan, Helio Salvatierra, Mili Smythe, and Ursula Wendel

1. My beautiful little daughter Sophie.
2. German engineered clown cars.
3. KrustyCon.
4. Extra-floppy shoes.
5. Banana peels. (Cheap, plentiful... always gets a laugh.)
6. Wetting my beak.
7. The rich cultural and religious heritage that is, whatchamacallit... Judaism.
8. The week John and Yoko cohosted my show.
9. The greatest chimp sidekick of them all, J. Fred Muggs.
10. Kablingy.
11. The smell of the greasepaint.
12. The roar of the crowd.
13. A great keister.
14. Tomfoolery.
15. Rigmarole.
16. Hijinks.
17. Johnnie Walker and his seafaring friend Captain Morgan.
18. Residual checks.
19. Tax shelters.
20. Calliope Rock.
21. Kickbacks.
22. The Borscht Belt.
23. Condor egg omelets.
24. Ten sweet little words: "We'll be right back after this word from our sponsor."
25. Cap'n Krusty's Not Quite Kosher Gefilte Fish Sticks™.
26. The sweet taste of a danish stolen from Kent Brockman.
27. A cigarette lit with a hundred dollar bill.
28. The Ed Ames "hatchet in the crotch" clip from "The Tonight Show."
29. Loopholes.
30. The drunken genius of Foster Brooks.
31. Dean Martin, the world's greatest straight man.
32. Jerry Lewis (with or without Dean Martin).
33. The gentle hum of my pacemaker.
34. Beating the odds.
35. Matt Groening's "Life in Hell." (Funny, funny strip. Man, I bet that guy's great to work for.)
36. Gazongas.
37. Bumblebee Man's annual Cinco de Mayo party.
38. Any of America's beautiful parks. (Santa Anita is my favorite.)
39. The secret language of Pig Latin.
40. My dear old Papa.

A DAY IN THE LIFE OF

10:00 a.m. - Wakes with hangover, pair of novelty fuzzy dice wrapped around his tongue. (Does not even want to know how they got there!)

10:30 a.m. - Time for breakfast. Orders Mr. Teeny to make him Bloody Mary. Smacks Mr. Teeny with newspaper for using Clamato. Heard yelling, "I could've had a V8!" repeatedly.

11:00 a.m. - Morning is not complete without three "S"s: schvitz/shower/shave.

11:45 a.m. - Runs nose through dishwasher until it is squeaky-clean.

12:30 p.m. - Arrives to cut ribbon at opening ceremony for another Krusty Clown House for Needy Kids—fun habitats with mirror-mazes/secret passageways/spooky mystery rooms.

12:35 p.m. - Denies reporter's allegation that some sick children wheeled into Krusty Clown House for Needy Kids are never heard from again.

1:00 p.m. - Drops clown car off at repair shop for brake job or louder horn—"whatever is cheaper." Later, mechanic discovers stowaways inside: two Little League baseball teams/ Springfield High School marching band.

1:30 p.m. - Walks into bar, says, "Give me a drink before my trouble starts." Bartender pours him drink. He quickly swallows it. "Give me another drink before my trouble starts," he says. Bartender complies. After gulping it down says, "Give me another before my trouble starts." As Krusty downs third drink, bartender says, "Hey, clown, when ya gonna pay for those drinks?" "Now my trouble starts!" he says, running for door.

2:00 p.m. - Arrives at Krustylu Studios to prepare for show. Stops to help security frisk female visitors/ pickpocket some spare change.

KRUSTY THE CLOWN

2:45 p.m. - Meets with licensee from latex company who wants to manufacture Krusty balloons. Gives man thumbs down, saying idea of balloons with his face is "too out there." Man says his company also makes condoms. "Sold!" Krusty says.

3:00 p.m. - Krusty's show starts. Today is "Fire Safety Day." (Special guests: Apu, chief of Springfield Volunteer Fire Department/fire-eater Otto/plastic explosives expert Snake.)

3:34 p.m. - Otto accidentally sets Sideshow Mel's hair on fire. Mel's frantic running around sets non-flame-retardant curtains on fire. When everyone looks to Apu for help, he says, "Don't look at me, Fire Chief is purely a figurehead position. But, I do make a damn fine firehouse Tandoori chicken!"

3:35 p.m. - As kids flee burning studio, Krusty reminds them of Message of the Day: "Stalking is the sincerest form of flattery." Which is why he doesn't understand Anna Kournikova making such a big deal about it.

3:36 p.m. - Snake walks away from fire disappointed Krusty would not let him show off plastic explosive skills. Very disappointed.

3:45 p.m. - Krusty hears sirens. Help is coming. Knowing he has warrant out for arrest, he hotfoots it to limo/heads for Springfield Downs racetrack.

3:50 p.m. - Complains to limo driver, Mr. Teeny, that all booze is gone from limo bar. Mr. Teeny explains yesterday was his cousin's bachelor party.

4:15 p.m. - Walks into Springfield Downs V.I.P. Bar with Mr. Teeny. Bartender points at sign. "Can't you read?" bartender growls. "'No Animals Allowed!'" Puts on sunglasses, pats Mr. Teeny's head. "I'm blind. This boy helps me see." "I never heard of a seeing-eye monkey before," bartender says. Acting flabbergasted, "They gave me a monkey?!"

4:30 p.m. - Racetrack promoters very pleased to see Krusty/need him to participate in today's special event: Celebrity Harness Racing. Since it is for charity, also owing them money, Krusty agrees to do it.

5:00 p.m. - Promoters show Krusty horse he will drive: #13 Apocalyptic. Previously scheduled celebrity driver dropped out for some reason—distinctive mark on horse's forehead that reads "666."

5:15 p.m. - Runs to place hefty bet on Apocalyptic. Likes 1000–1 odds.

5:30 p.m. - Takes a look at other celebrity harness drivers: Bumblebee Man, Arnie Pie, Miss Springfield, Duffman, Rainier Wolfcastle's alcoholic ex-brother-in-law. Runs to increase bet.

5:45 p.m. - As race is about to begin, he gives Apocalyptic a special cocktail of vitamins, caffeine, steroids, Xanax. Hopes it works, since he was planning on taking it as pick-me-up later (before some kid's birthday party).

5:50 p.m. - They're off! After seven thrilling minutes zig-zagging around track, Apocalyptic comes in last, but gives crowd demonstration of healthy bowels while trotting. From sulky, Krusty gets first-hand look.

6:00 p.m. - Turns out Apocalyptic belongs to Fat Tony, who is upset Krusty gave his racehorse drugs. Mobsters meet to decide payback. Cutting off horse's head/putting it in Krusty's bed suggested—rejected for being counter-productive and derivative. Finally, they just decide to shoot the clown.

6:10 p.m. - Krusty leaves racetrack. He has Mr. Teeny drive limo through car wash/rides on roof to get cleaned up

6:15 p.m. - Fat Tony's boys arrive/riddle Krusty's limo with hundred rounds of bullets. Strangely, they all aim for front passenger tire.

6:20 p.m. - Krusty/Mr. Teeny unharmed. They deploy emergency getaway vehicle. (Mr. Teeny fetches tiny tricycle from trunk.) Flee scene before mobsters realize they are gone—albeit slowly, with lots of squeaky wheel noise.

6:22 p.m. - Mobsters approach limo to finish job/argue who had "dibs" on front passenger tire. They spot Krusty/Mr. Teeny on tricycle half-block away.

6:23 p.m. - Plastic explosive on undercarriage of limo explodes, scattering mobsters onto nearby houses/neighborhood bushes.

6:25 p.m. - Krusty/Mr. Teeny, still on tricycle, get stuck behind marching band/kids in baseball uniforms trying to find their way home. Soon, people line street, thinking it is parade.

6:35 p.m. - Tired of pedaling, Krusty parks. He/Mr. Teeny go into bar/order ten whiskey shots. Bartender looks on as they quickly down four whiskeys (each in less than a minute). "You shouldn't drink those so fast," bartender says. "You would, if you had what we have," Krusty says, as they throw back fifth drink. "What do you have?" bartender asks. "Fifty cents!" Krusty puts spare change on bar/runs out with Mr. Teeny.

7:00 p.m. - Arrives at birthday party where he is supposed to perform for little wiener kid with glasses/big nose. Some kid named Bart claims to know him. Whatever.

7:10 p.m. - After ten minutes of balloon animals/"knock-knock" jokes, Krusty slumps to floor, relating current woes to partygoers. Mr. Teeny chatters about how he is down to his last Cuban cigar/ lights up/blames Republicans.

7:15 p.m. - Depressed clown/smoking monkey can only amuse kids for so long. Prepubescent catcalls/garbage throwing ensue.

7:20 p.m. - Fat Tony/mobsters show up/shoot bullets. Krusty does amazing acrobatics to avoid death. Kids are now entertained.

7:25 p.m. - Explosions go off on front lawn, scattering mobsters. Kids cheer what they think is fireworks show. Snake heard yelling, "Take that, clown dude! Now, give back my fuzzy dice!"

7:35 p.m. - Soon police cars/ambulances arrive. Colored flashing lights bring tears of joy to birthday boy's eyes.

7:36 p.m. - ??? - Krusty crawls behind wiener boy's father's wet bar/starts drinking heavily/ stays there until blotto. (When he wakes up with hangover next morning, does not even want to know how he got there!)

Li'L KRUSTY

KRUSTY THE CLOWN'S OFFICIAL APPEARANCE RIDER
CONGRATULATIONS, YOU'VE GOT KRUSTY!

You or your organization is having Krusty the Clown appear in conjunction with an upcoming event! Either you've hired Krusty, Krusty is participating under the terms of a court settlement, or Krusty is working for you as a part of one of his current community service sentences! Please copy, distribute, and review this with all event staff members: This document will give instructions on the various protocols that need to be followed to ensure Krusty's comfort, state of mind, and safety—not to mention the safety of others. The difference between a hilarious fun-filled event or a tear-filled "incident" that requires a police report is this document!

Stage Requirements
- Elevated 10' X 10' stage
- Working microphone
- Portable defibrillator within five feet of Krusty at all times

Props
- Ribbon cuttings: oversized scissors at least five times, but no greater than ten times, the size of normal scissors
- Boat christenings: one bottle of non-alcoholic champagne (Krusty WILL NOT use alcohol for anything else but drinking), pre-cracked for easy breakage
- Krusty's "Old West 'Meringue 'Em High at Pie Noon' Showdown Show": twenty-seven Krusty Brand® "Throwin' Pies" (Banana Crème-flavored)

Krusty's Dressing Room
This room should comfortably hold four people and a chimpanzee and contain:
- A vibrating, leather, recliner chair and three, hard, metal folding chairs
- A television with either satellite or digital cable, capable of receiving the Dog Racing Channel
- Four Dominican cigars
- Twenty-four bottles of cold bottled water (not KRUSTANI™)
- A size ten fez
- Three pounds of organic bananas
- A carving station and chef. (The chef should not be STINGY with the AU JUS.) A glass should be provided for "gravy shots."
- Sixteen Boston Crème donuts
- A chafing dish filled with bacon and sausage (not KRUSTYLOIN™)
- Ten bottles of brandy
- Ten bottles of seltzer
- Ten bottles of Krusty Brand® "Non-Potable Seltzer for Soakin' Saps"
- A giant bowl of "'nanner puddin'"
- Two tins of clown shoe polish
- A package of chimp diapers
- Smelling salts
- A loaded gun and an expendable television set

SPECIAL REQUESTS
- In the event that Krusty passes out, he must be turned to lie on his side.
- Do not make direct eye contact with Krusty, unless it's to compliment him on his brilliant career.
- Please do not feed chili to Krusty's chimpanzee, Mr. Teeny.

IN THE EVENT OF KRUSTY'S DEATH
Please remove all evidence from the immediate area. (Even if Krusty is not directly responsible for his own demise, questions will lead to other questions that the members of "Team Krusty" just don't want to answer.) Please also remove:
- Any "nudie" mags
- Evidence of business dealings with rogue nations
- Escort receipts
- Pirated DVDs
- Endangered animal pelts

Please take note that your down payment will not be refunded, even if Krusty's death occurs before the show.

AND, MOST IMPORTANT...relax, forget about any potential liability resulting from minor infractions of this rider, and have a Krustabulous time!

THE KRUSTYLU STUDIOS EXECUTIVE OFFICE!

1. The Big Ratings Board. ("Oy. Last week we got beat by a laxative infomercial.")
2. Sideshow Mel Action Cannon Playset™. ("Same old story: Some kid gets blasted in the eye with a plastic action figure of your sidekick and suddenly **you're** the bad guy.")
3. Krusty Wall Clock with Extra-Long Tongue Pendulum™. ("Taken off the market when Gene Simmons sued for copyright infringement.")
4. Krusty-Keeps-It-Krispy Lunchbox™. ("Great idea: Managing moisture levels in lunchboxes with standard humidor technology. Bad idea: Using lead-based paint because it was the closest match for 'Krustyhair Green.'")
5. Krusty Plaque Blaster Electric Toothbrusher™. "Okay...it ripped gums. Sue me. Yeah, you probably did."
6. Krusty's "Hey, Hey!" Talking Alarm Clock™. ("A rare collectible. The voice chip was so loud and obnoxious that most of these were smashed against bedroom walls.")
7. "Kroon Along with Krusty!" gold record. ("Featuring my famous duet with Harvey Fierstein on 'When the Swallows Come Back to Capistrano.'")
8. The Krusty Talking Doll™. ("We offered it with a 'no snapback' guarantee and moved 2 million units. I freakin' love this doll. A lot of people say I should've stopped with the merchandizing right there. I tell those people I can't hear 'em...I have thousand dollar bills stuffed in my ears.")
9. Marble bust given to me by the nation of France. ("They couldn't help but surrender to my comedy!")
10. Poster for the first Krusty telethon. ("Cash was raised. Stuff was cured. It was one of the most selfless things I've ever done. Money can't buy that kind of exposure!")
11. Krusty's Bombs-Away Firecracker Thrower™. ("For a while, it was the best firecracker thrower on the market.")
12. Off-brand booze in unmarked, square, crystal decanters. ("Classy.")
13. Cabinet purchased at Glen Campbell's yard sale.
14. Coffee table. ("Jason Hervey, that kid from "The Wonder Years," owed me some money. He was a little short, so he gave me his coffee table. That guy is a class act. He obviously knows how to use a coaster.")

After a dishonorable discharge from the space program, Mr. Teeny joined "The Krusty the Clown Show," where, in exchange for his recklessly entertaining roller skating, he gets to wear a little hat and smoke cigars. More than just a one-trick-panzee, Mr. Teeny also rides a tricycle, attends to Krusty's last minute grooming needs, occasionally writes Krusty's material, and can perform an alarmingly effective striptease to the propulsive strains of sweet funk music.

- **Quote:** "Ook-ook!"

- **Description:** Small, hairy, and simian.
- **Demeanor:** Deceptively cute.
- **Secret shame:** Has a deathly fear of trees.
- **Claim to fame:** Using Krusty's credit card and a touch-tone phone, he can place bets at the track.
- **Likes:** Cohiba Siglo IVs, Montecristo #2s, and screwing around with the car radio.
- **Dislikes:** Organ grinders, Hurdy-Gurdy Men, network executives, and dogs that walk on their hind legs.
- **Special skills:** Can tie his own bow tie and drive a stick shift.
- **Secret ambition:** To one day have his own talk show.
- **Favorite foods:** Chocolate ice cream, head lice, and nicotine gum.
- **Awards:** Named "Smoking Chimp of the Year" by the National Tobacco Board.
- **Didja know:** Bart once considered Mr. Teeny a potential boyfriend for Mrs. Krabappel.

I'M TIRED OF HIS SHOWBOATING. NO CHIMP'S GONNA MAKE A MONKEY OUTTA ME! *GET IT*? CHIMP? MONKEY?!

Sideshow Mel is a consummate professional. Despite being shot out of a cannon, sawed in half, engulfed in fire, swarmed by flea-bitten kazoo-brandishing monkeys, or having his buttocks frozen with liquid nitrogen and cracked with a hammer, Mel always strives to maintain his dignity. When not enduring Krusty's employment, Mel enjoys the company of his pet Afghan Cornelius and hanging out with his companion Barbara at the Pimento Grove, after which, if he's lucky, she will pleasure him with the French Arts.

- **Quote:** "Oh, Krusty! You can be so cruel when you're sober!"

- **Real name:** Melvin Van Horne.
- **Alter ego:** Sideshow Melanie.
- **Education:** Adult Education Annex and Cornell University.
- **Meteorological prowess:** He can predict the weather using the bone in his topknot.
- **Instrumental talent:** Plays both the slide whistle and the bicycle horn and is the conductor for the Monkeytown Philharmonic.
- **Likes:** Graham crackers, "Robert's Rules of Order," and the unsettling tenor magic of Jim Nabors.
- **Dislikes:** Sloppy grammar, hootenannies, and anything that might harm the sky, because "that's where clouds are born."
- **Organizational affiliations:** The Stonecutters, Toastmasters, Alcoholics Anonymous, and a lifetime membership with the American Kennel Club.
- **Celebrity status:** Featured in the "We're Sending Our Love Down the Well" celebrity sing-a-thon, is a regular on "Springfield Squares," and has his own parking space.

SIDESHOW MEL IS POSSIBLY MY MOST ENTERTAINING SIDEKICK, ESPECIALLY WHEN HE'S WACKED-OUT ON WOWIE-SAUCE!

MISS LOIS PENNYCANDY KRUSTY'S PERSONAL ASSISTANT

Miss Lois Pennycandy is an attractive, intelligent, resourceful woman with advanced degrees in Art History and Mathematics. As such, she is well qualified to assist Krusty with the important work of massaging his ego, retrieving his dry-cleaning, sweet-talking his bookie, and wrestling him into his tux. Miss Pennycandy carries a torch for Krusty the Clown. Her eyes light up whenever he enters the room. Sadly, the only thing she lights up for Krusty is his cigar.

- **Quote:** "Krusty is a maddening impossible man. I've wasted my womanhood wondering how he can hurt someone who loves him so."

- **Dress:** Stylish and professional.
- **Demeanor:** Polite, harried, and annoyed.
- **Lipstick:** Pink and glossy.
- **Adornments:** Red pearl choker and earrings.
- **Other responsibilities:** Answering phones, apologizing for Krusty's offensive remarks, keeping the bar well stocked, and reminding Krusty how brilliant he is.
- **Claim to fame:** Can keep five people on hold simultaneously.
- **Secret shame:** She likes it when Krusty talks clowny to her.
- **Office wall decor:** Pictures of Krusty with The Beatles, Krusty and Alfred Hitchcock sitting in each others' directors chairs, and Krusty wrestling Lou Ferrigno as the Incredible Hulk.

MISS PENNYCANDY WORKS HARDER THAN ANY THREE PEOPLE I KNOW. THE BEAUTY PART IS I ONLY HAVE TO PAY ONE SALARY.

SIDESHOW BOB CRIMINAL MASTERMIND AND FORMER SECOND BANANA TO KRUSTY THE CLOWN

While accompanying younger brother Cecil to one of Krusty's auditions, Bob's innate genius was accidentally discovered—a genius for being hit in the face by pies. Thus, Sideshow Bob became a Krusty regular, playing the slide whistle, absorbing the hurling of countless pies, and being shot from the mouth of a cannon, repeatedly. With a desire to steer his career toward literate whimsy and away from vulgar slapstick, Bob framed Krusty for murder, temporarily gaining control of the show—and launching a fantastic criminal career, much of it devoted to murdering Krusty and Bart Simpson.

- **Quote:** "My foolish capering destroyed more young minds than syphilis and pinball combined."

- **Real name:** Robert Underdunk Terwilliger.
- **Krusty's first nickname for Bob:** Lord Autumnbottom.
- **Places of incarceration:** Springwood Minimum Security Prison, Springfield Penitentiary, Campbell's Chunky Soup Maximum Security Prison.
- **Prison work detail:** Earns 5 cents an hour raking up condom wrappers at local military bases.
- **Prison recreations:** Building Westminster Abbey in a bottle, reading "Prison Bride" magazine, and writing haiku while skinheads beat him with soap.
- **Likes:** Decent local marmalade, scrimshaw, Cole Porter songs, a well-balanced shampoo, and the versatility of dynamite.
- **Dislikes:** Garden rakes, Tom Clancy books, prison-issue shower sandals, and the omni-directional sludge pump known as television.

EVERY TIME SIDESHOW BOB TRIES TO KILL ME, MY RATINGS GO THROUGH THE ROOF!

An intensely private man, Corporal Punishment is Krusty the Clown's sergeant-at-arms. As captain of his neighborhood watch, he spends the major part of his leisure time poking his nose into other people's affairs, but, in general, he's a loner. In addition to protecting Krusty from any unscripted contact with children, Corporal Punishment runs valuable interference with network executives, OSHA inspectors, bookies, and IRS agents.

- **Quote:** (Classified.)

- **Dress:** Combat ready.
- **Demeanor:** Stern and forbidding.
- **Manner:** Silent but deadly.
- **Likes:** Cotton candy, long walks on the beach, and snuggling.
- **Dislikes:** Anyone who mentions he likes cotton candy, long walks on the beach, and snuggling.
- **Secret shame:** Not a real corporal. His flat feet prevented him from ever serving in the military.
- **Claim to fame:** Once went 127 days without speaking.
- **Hobbies:** Kickboxing, power lifting, bull riding, and collecting butterflies.
- **Employment history:** Bronco buster, bouncer, mattress tester.
- **Special skills:** Crushes bricks with his bare hands, expert long-range marksman, and makes exquisite gelato.

DON'T WORRY. WHEN HE'S HUSTLING SOME AUTOGRAPH-HUNGRY LITTLE PISHER OUT OF MY SIGHT, HE MAY SEEM ANGRY, BUT HE'S REALLY LAUGHING INSIDE.

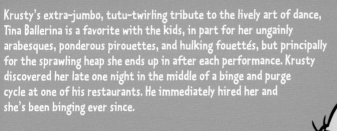

TINA BALLERINA FEATURED DANCER ON "THE KRUSTY THE CLOWN SHOW"

Krusty's extra-jumbo, tutu-twirling tribute to the lively art of dance, Tina Ballerina is a favorite with the kids, in part for her ungainly arabesques, ponderous pirouettes, and hulking fouettés, but principally for the sprawling heap she ends up in after each performance. Krusty discovered her late one night in the middle of a binge and purge cycle at one of his restaurants. He immediately hired her and she's been binging ever since.

- **Quote:** "Krusty really helped awaken my appetite for performing."

- **Hair:** Upswept, dramatic, and dyed.
- **Eyelashes:** Long and fluttery.
- **Dress:** Tutu and unitard.
- **Least favorite routine:** The Dancing Piñata.
- **Favorite meal:** Krusty Burger Beef-Flavored Chicken Sandwich.™
- **Fondest dream:** To one day have a sandwich named after her.
- **Favorite pastimes:** Collecting pancakes, flying kites, and opposable thumb wrestling with Mr. Teeny.
- **Mortal enemy:** Little Vicki Valentine.
- **Her performing secret:** What she lacks in grace she makes up for in determination.

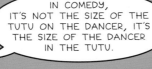

IN COMEDY, IT'S NOT THE SIZE OF THE TUTU ON THE DANCER, IT'S THE SIZE OF THE DANCER IN THE TUTU.

Despite the fact Krusty can't remember his name, Bart is given the coveted job of assistant—not because he saved Krusty from jail, reunited him with his estranged father, or saved his career by organizing a comeback special—but because he got him a danish. After accidently poisoning Sideshow Mel, Bart fills in for Mel on camera, destroying the set and inadvertently achieving fame as the "I Didn't Do It!" Boy.

- **Quote:** "Show business sucks."

- **The duties of an assistant:** Being on call 24/7, washing towels, picking up dry cleaning, feeding the cast, cleaning toilets, getting yelled at, signing Krusty's autographs, and putting your own fingerprints on incriminating evidence to provide Krusty with alibis.
- **Krusty's nicknames for Bart:** "Yutz," "little pisher," and "my gold-plated shlemiel."
- **"I Didn't Do It!" related ventures:** A rap CD "I Didn't Do It! Vol. III," a biography "I Didn't Do It! The Bart Simpson Story," the "I Didn't Do It!" Dancers, Bart Chat phone service, and the "I Didn't Do It!" Boy promotional tour ($5 per viewing).
- **Krusty's shpiel:** "See the boy that says the words you've been longing to hear, like the salivating dogs that you are!"
- **Selected "I Didn't Do It!" sketches:** The Ming Vase on the Ladder Sketch, The Giant House of Cards Sketch, The Leaning Tower of Pizzas Sketch, The Plate Spinning Tight Rope Sketch, The Disarming the Nuclear Bomb Sketch, and The William Tell Sketch.
- **Homer's alternative catch phrases:** "Bucka bucka" and "Woozle wozzle."
- **Haste makes dubious taste:** "I Didn't Do It! The Bart Simpson Story" is mostly about Ross Perot and the last two chapters are excerpts from the Oliver North trial.

> SHOW BUSINESS IS A DREAM FACTORY, BART, THE BIRTHPLACE OF MAGIC AND ENCHANTMENT. NOW I NEED YOU TO GO AND CLEAN OUT MY TOILET.

Distressed by questions, disrespected by multitudes, disowned by his own mother, the Squeaky-Voiced Teen (a.k.a. the Pimple-Faced Kid, a.k.a. Old Man Peterson) is an ineptly reliable Krusty Burger employee. He also may be one of our nation's most vital natural resources as, according to Homer, there must be $20 of grease on his forehead alone. His biggest work responsibility to date is making sure enough mayonnaise is left out in the sun to make Krusty's Special Sauce.

- **Quote:** "Every mistake comes out of my salary. If I had a girlfriend, she'd kill me."

- **Dress:** Ill-fitting uniform and hat (as the job dictates).
- **Demeanor:** Uneasy and skittish.
- **Complexion:** Wan, greasy, and acne-ridden.
- **Mom:** Lunchlady Doris.
- **Related fast-food experience:** Gulp 'n' Blow, Lard Lad Donuts, IRS Burger, Shakespeare's Fried Chicken, and TacoMat.
- **Other employment:** Stock boy at Eatie Gourmet's Health Food Store and Kidstown USA, change boy at Noiseland Arcade, Springfield Barber College trainee, parking jockey at the Springfield Air Show and Springfield War Memorial Stadium, car wash cashier, ticket seller at the Springfield Googolplex, tour guide at the Springfield Wax Museum, Springfield International Airport security checker, Mr. Burns' Casino hospitality, Springfield Public Access Channel 3, and Clumsy Student Movers.
- **References:** Mr. Marouka at Krusty Burger, Mr. Johansson at the Gulp 'n' Blow, Mr. Wise at Kidstown USA (not affiliated with Kidstown Juvenile Correction Farm), and Mr. Wembley at the Agricultural Inspection Checkpoint.
- **Awards:** Received three medals from the US Air Force for his heroic parking skills.

YOU NEED TO FIND THE RIGHT TOOL FOR THE JOB. AND THAT'S WHY THIS ENTRY-LEVEL MINIMUM WAGE TOOL SELLS MY MEAT-FLAVORED SANDWICHES.

HEY, KIDS! IS YOUR DIALOGUE STRAIGHT OUTTA DULLSVILLE? WHEN YOU TALK, DO THE DAMES WALK? PUT A LITTLE LIFE IN YOUR LINGO, SOME GET-UP-AND-GO IN YOUR GAB, AND ADD OODLES OF OOMPH TO YOUR ORATORY WITH...

Krusty's
THESAURUS OF
BACKSTAGE SLANG

BEFORE
1. Excuse me, miss, is this seat taken?
2. Please, allow me to pay for dinner.

AFTER
1. Hey, hey, sweet patootie! Mind if I park my carcass here?
2. Strap on the feed bag, baby. This chowfest is on me!

HERE'S AN EXCERPT FROM THIS DESTINED-TO-BE CLASSIC REFERENCE BOOK!

362. Other Denizens of the Theatre 1. *COMEDIAN* - Baggy-pants man, banana, belly buster, buffoon, farceur, foil, fool, gagman, hambone, jokesmith, jokester, kibitzer, madcap, merry-andrew, mime, mountebank, mummer, panic, prankster, quipster, riot, scream, screwball, sidesplitter, stooge, wisecracker. 2. *PATRON* - Cash customer, chump, down-fronter, fish, ham-and-egger, hick, John Q. Public, local yokel, matinee mamma, natives, palooka, plush bottom, stargazer, sucker. 3. *HANGER ON* - Dead battery, deadhead, excess baggage, flat tire, gate crasher, goldbrick, hangover, lollygagger, lounge lizard, moocher, schnorer, sponge, stage door Johnny, wallflower. 4. *AGENT* - Ballyhoo man, bird dog, biz rep, fixer, flesh peddler, handler, headache man, ten-percenter. 5. *CRITIC* - Act catcher, boogie man, crick, drammer damner, the Death Watch, log roller.

519. Broads 1. *SWELL DAME* (terms of endearment) - Babe, bachelor bait, beauty, cheesecake, chick, cutsie, cutsie-tootsie, doll, filly, fox, frail, gal, honey bunny, live wire, mama, she, sister, skirt, sweet patootie, tomato, toots, trixie, the weaker sex. 2. *LOUSY BROAD* (terms of disparagement) - Ball and chain, battle-axe, bimbo, clock stopper, cold shoulder, dill pickle, flighty frill, fried egg, gold digger, half sister to a shot of dynamite, old bat, pain in the atlas. 3. *CHORUS GIRL* - Boot rattler, burley cutie, cement mixer, follie dolly, floor mopper, hoofer, hootchie-cootcher, leg shaker, step-sister.

DON'T WAIT FOR THE REMAINDERS! RESERVE A COPY AT YOUR FAVORITE BOOK SHOP OR DISCOUNT WAREHOUSE TODAY!

Li'L KRUSTY

SIDESHOW RAHEEM:
THE REVOLUTION WAS BRIEFLY TELEVISED

1989. A new, proud, afrocentric, cultural movement has sprung up and the media reflects it. The year sees the release of Public Enemy's breakthrough anthem "Fight the Power" and Spike Lee's *Do the Right Thing*. Africa medallions swing from the necks of millions of college students. And the nation is captivated by a young actor on "A Different World" with flip-down sunglasses by the name of Kadeem Hardison.

> ## "Angry, angry young man."
> —Krusty the Clown,
> describing Sideshow Raheem

Left: Sideshow Raheem early promotional poster.
Above: Sideshow Raheem joins the "Krusty" cast.
Opposite: Rare glimpse of early on-set problems between Raheem and Krusty.

The world is changing, and Krusty the Clown senses it. Whether it was a benevolent act of diversity or a cynical, calculated play to capitalize on a trend, Krusty hires Raheem Banjoko (*nee* Russell Mason) to be his sidekick. Raheem is a recent graduate of the historically black Mission College, where he had a morning radio show, "Raheem's Nubian Sunrise Jammy Jam." The show combined messages of afrocentrism and Black Pride with crank calls to liquor stores and vegan pie-throwing comedy. Raheem Banjoko becomes Sideshow Raheem, and a new day begins on "The Krusty the Clown Show."

INITIAL PROBLEMS

"It was not a good first day," an unnamed Krustylu exec recalls. "Krusty's first bit for Raheem was an 'Oh My Goshage it's Krusty Brand® Sausage!' live ad spot. Raheem looked at the script and simply said, 'Oh, hell no.'" Being a devout member of the Nation of Islam, Raheem refused to promote the consumption of pork products. Krusty reasoned that he himself had no problem with shilling sausage and bacon, despite his "Jewishesque" background. An argument erupted. It ended with Krusty's head tied up in sausage casing.

"Things went downhill from there," the exec says. "Raheem wanted to control the portrayal of his 'character' very carefully. He told Krusty that he was trying to 'redefine sideshowhood as people know it—making it more about freeing oneself from the oppression of a white-faced clown.' When Krusty heard that...well, he just plotzed."

Raheem refused to be fired from a cannon, wear anything in his hair, or even dress up like an infant for the "Li'l Krusty" skit. Instead, he would sit onstage, silently judging Krusty for the majority of the broadcast, occasionally reading some of his "modern" poetry, quoting Cornel West, or holding up various signs featuring phrases such as "Africans Invented Civilization."

A SUDDEN END

One week after he was hired, an incident took place in which Sideshow Raheem threw Krusty through the show's clown car. It is unclear to this day whether this occurrence precipitated Raheem's departure or was the direct result of a dispute stemming from the announcement of his resignation from the show.

Above: Krusty on Dutch television.
Right: Sideshow Raheem makes a
statement with his graduation portrait.

During an appearance on Dutch televison five years ago, Krusty, who was, at best, drunk during the interview, had this to say:

"I made that kid. I plucked him out of podunk college radio and gave him a chance to run with the big-shoe boys...So one day, he read me this whiny poem about how high-top sneakers are just a modern day chain gang manacle for a new generation of slaves. That reminded me of a joke. So I asked him if he ever heard the one about the plantation owner's illegitimate slave daughter and the traveling whip salesman. Next thing I know, I'm flyin' through the Jokeswagon!"

> ## "I made that kid."
>
> -Krusty the Clown, on
> Sideshow Raheem

But there are other reports of what happened that day. Some say Krusty, annoyed at his new sidekick's inflexibility, spiked Raheem's lentil soup with bacon. Others say Krusty tried his hand at a "yo' mama" joke. Perhaps the most credible explanation of the incident portrays Raheem's act as one of self-defense.

Recently unearthed documents reveal that Raheem (who declined to be interviewed for this article) was offered a position at Morehouse College as a professor of Media Studies, shortly before leaving "The Krusty the

Clown Show." It is believed that Raheem may have only joined the show as a part of his doctoral thesis entitled, "Go Tell It on the Clowntaintop: Being an African Americlown Sidekick." Supposedly, when Raheem resigned and disclosed his academic ulterior motives, Krusty became violent, trying to hit Raheem with an oversized tube of toothpaste. Raheem immediately subdued the agitated headliner. Krusty skulked off, only to return some time later, drunk and behind the wheel of the Jokeswagon, where he attempted to run Raheem over. Krusty missed, spinning out of control on a banana peel and wrapping the clown car around a giant Easter Island totem bearing his likeness.

WHERE IS HE NOW?

Raheem Banjoko ended his association with Morehouse College after the institution refused

to publish his book, *Rerun Was a Sellout: Militancy in "What's Happening Now!"* and promptly withdrew from public life. Rumors abound as to his current whereabouts. Others report of Raheem spending the last ten years living in Maine, performing a daily version of his own children's show that he refuses to broadcast, tape, or even perform in front of a live audience.

INDELIBLE IMPACT

Regardless of whatever Raheem is doing now, his albeit brief contribution to "The Krusty the Clown Show" is the stuff of legend—the collision of his militant, uncompromising, sidekick-that-refuses-to-be-kicked-around persona with Krusty's apolitical, gleefully self-serving huckster was a festival of awkward discomfort that threatened to explode at any moment. Recently, curiosity regarding Raheem led to the first ever "Sideshow Raheem Conny Con" in the Maple Banquet Room of the Clark, New Jersey, Ramada Inn. Krusty, sensing an opportunity to cash in on the newfound interest in his old foe/sidekick is readying a DVD release of *The Krusty the Clown Show: The Best of Sideshow Raheem*, of which he was heard to recently remark on radio station KBBL's "Bill & Marty's Morning Zoo": "He was angry, and yeah, he threw me into a car...but, oy, I gotta admit, the boy had something...Did I say 'boy'? I meant 'man.' Man! Oh, holy crap. I hope he's not listening."

Top Left: Krusty's attempt to run over Raheem results in an embarrassing wipe-out
Bottom Left: Cover of the upcoming *Best of Sideshow Raheem* DVD.

Let's see what's happening inside...
KRUSTY'S JOKE VAULT

KRUSTYLU STUDIOS

MEMO

To: My easily replaced writing staff
From: Krusty
Re: Restocking the Joke Vault

I bought these jokes at Bob Hope's estate sale. Read over my notes (in red) and see what you dimwits can do to punch them up and "Krustify" them.

-Krusty

P.S. It has come to my attention that some of you have been eating lunch during your lunch hour. Need I remind you of "The Krusty the Clown Show's" policy of zero tolerance for funny business? Knock it off and get back to work.

Hey, hey! [laugh] meshugeneh
∧ So, how about those hippies, huh? I saw a couple the other

day. One of them had hair down to here. And that was the guy!
Get it? The guy had longer hair than the gal!

Hippies! I saw one drown last week. The lifeguard couldn't

save him because he was too far out, man!

Hoo hoo hoo ha ha ha haw!
∧ Doctors! I asked my doctor, "Doctor, will this ointment clear

up my spots?" So the doctor says, "I never make rash

promises!" So sue me, already!

And how about all these farkakte credit cards, huh? [wait for laugh] Someone stole all my credit cards, but I didn't report it. The thief spends less than my ex-wife does. You see? My ex-wife rips me off more than the guy who stole my credit cards!

The last time I played golf with President Ford he hit a birdie—and an eagle, a moose, an elk, an aardvark...

(Update this one: change Ford to Nixon and change the aardvark to a hippie.)

So, how about that food they serve you on airplanes, huh? I just flew in from New York, and boy, am I hungry! [wait for laugh] Airlines! The other thing about airlines, even if you don't have reservations, you have reservations! You don't have reservations for the flight but you have reservations about flying.

HEY, HEY!
You hear the one about the birds and the bees? My father told me all about the birds and the bees—I went steady with a blue jay till I was twenty-one.

MY FATHER!
Don't get me started. Such a putz you never met!

Eisenhower isn't worried about the Russians dropping the bomb! [wait for laugh] One false move and he'll drop Joe McCarthy on Moscow!

(Update this one: change Eisenhower to whoever is president now and change Joe McCarthy to a funnier name, Joe Schmoe or something. And change Moscow to a funny sounding city, like Schenectady or Altoona.)

Yessir, folks...and what about this Woman's Liberation Movement? Where else but in America could these wacky lady libbers take off their bras then complain about their lack of support? (Classic! Leave it as is!)

Here it is, finally unearthed for your perusal! This is the book Krusty fans have yearned to read and government officials have subpoenaed to acquire! Think being a KRUSTY BURGER™ worker is a walk in the park? Think again after you read…

THE FIRST TWO PAGES OF THE
KRUSTY BURGER™ EMPLOYEES MANUAL!

CONGRATULATIONS! YOU'RE A KRUSTY BURGER™ MEISTER!

IT IS NOW YOUR SACRED PRIVILEGE TO SERVE UP GRADE-C MEAT WITH A GRADE-A ATTITUDE!

YOUR TASK ABOVE ALL OTHERS IS TO KNOW HOW TO DO THE FOLLOWING:

MAKE "FRIENDS" WITH THE HEALTH INSPECTOR!

Whenever an official from the Health Department arrives at KRUSTY BURGER™, he/she is ALWAYS to be met with a KRUSTY BURGER™ SUPREME ($500 sandwiched between two sesame seed buns).

WHAT YOU NEED TO KNOW ABOUT THE CUSTOMER:

1 The customer is a human being with an immune system: he/she can certainly digest food that has been dropped on the floor.

2 The customer is someone who does not want to be burdened with having to know exactly what kind of meat is in an "all-meat" hamburger.

3 You can't spell "customer" without **us** and **me**, so don't forget the order of importance in any dispute with buying public.

4 The customer is not really a customer until they have paid for their food. When they give you the money, you give them the respect.

GET TO KNOW...

THE KRUSTY SECRET MENU!

These items are not on the regular KRUSTY BURGER™ menu, but die-hard KB fanatics will occasionally ask for them. It's best not to upset these freaks —so be prepared!

"Veggie" Burger
Specially-dyed meat patty, made to look vegetarian.

Crouton Burger
A KRUSTY BURGER™ on a two-week-old bun.

Fries – Well Done
An order of french fries, stuck into half a Buzz Cola can, doused in grease, and lit on fire.

Wrongway Corrigan
Half a bun put between two burgers.

Insano-Style
Fifteen KRUSTY BURGER™ patties tied up in licorice rope and then deep fried.

THE KRUSTY BURGER™ GAME FACE!

WRONG!
Depressed?
Sullen?
Full of teenage angst?

NOT ON THE CLOCK, JUNIOR!

RIGHT!
Pretend that if you don't smile, your family is gonna get roughed up! Remember the three **P**s! **P**eepers, **P**osture, **P**early whites—and the personal safety of your loved ones is ensured!

YOUR FUTURE
IN THE KRUSTY BURGER™ ORGANIZATION

Listen…here's the deal. I've started negotiations with a company called Taipei Food Service Robotics. Now, it's gonna be a few years until I have the Tin Man flipping burgers, but it's coming, and the actual humans I'm keeping on are gonna be the ones with a commitment to excellence; the ones that know the difference between leanin' and cleanin'; the ones that sweat the details but don't sweat all over the food. So stay on your toes! Your robot bosses are gonna be a lot less forgiving than me.

KRUSTY'S HOT 100 DOCTOR'S ORDERS

1. Do not wear big floppy clown shoes for more than 45 minutes a day.
2. Avoid all activities that hurt only when you laugh.
3. Limit bow ties to 150% above normal size.
4. Avoid trying in vain to sweep a circle of light into the trash and other stressful activities.
5. Avoid loud and sudden noises, including but not limited to the laughter of children.
6. Avoid children.
7. Also cute animals.
8. Avoid sugar.
9. Avoid caffeine.
10. Avoid Krusty Farms™ Caffeinated Sugar.
11. AVOID ALL KRUSTY BRAND® FOODS. (I say this to everyone!)
12. Avoid fat.
13. Avoid lard.
14. Avoid blubber.
15. Avoid Homer Simpson.
16. Limit daily food intake to 1,500 calories.
17. If you consume more than 1,500 calories, induce vomiting immediately.
18. Repeat as necessary.
19. Don't get pudding in your eye.
20. (Sorry, that last one was meant for Lenonardson.)

21. Take 20MG placebo six times a day.
22. Apply skin cream after contact with fur-bearing mammals.
23. Apply skin gel after contact with scaly reptiles.
24. Apply skin powder after contact with leafy plants.
25. Apply cold to eyes after prolonged exposure to reds and yellows.
26. Apply lip balm to inside of underwear.
27. Apply nicotine patch (EXTERNALLY this time).
28. There is no such thing as an alcohol patch (so stop asking).
29. Soak dentures overnight in solution of cough syrup and wart remover.
30. Keep the inside of your mouth clean and dry.
31. Boil all clothing.
32. Do not touch a thing.
33. Just go sit in the yard until the plastic furniture covers arrive.
34. Complain about how rotten it is to get older.
35. Take these feelings out on young people.
36. Let me know if the pacemaker I installed in your chest is working all right...
37. ...Because I can't find my iPod.
38. Just in case it's really a pacemaker, avoid microwave ovens.
39. Avoid costumed heroes with super-magnetism powers.
40. Avoid strobe lights.
41. Avoid direct sunlight.
42. Avoid sudden shocks.
43. Avoid severe electrical shocks.
44. If severe electrical shocks persist for more than four hours, seek immediate medical treatment.
45. Do not take knives or bullets internally.
46. Wise up.
47. Get on your knees and beg the heavens to forgive you for every rotten thing you've done.
48. Get up and bandage your knees. (Kneeling is the worst thing for them.)
49. If humours get out of balance, try bloodletting.
50. (Sorry, that last one was meant for Mr. Burns.)
51. Avoid beverages that make you loud, silly, or angry.
52. If you must chew tobacco, do not light it.
53. This applies also to bubble gum that looks like chewing tobacco.
54. In fact, avoid all bubble gum that looks like anything that's not bubble gum.
55. Bubble gum that looks like itself is bad enough.
56. WATER must be boiled.
57. AIR must be conditioned.
58. EARTH must be destroyed.
59. FIRE is the fourth element.
60. (SPOILER:) The fifth element is LOVE.

61. Walk three hours a week.
62. Riding a golf cart is not walking.
63. Meditate 15 minutes a day.
64. Looking at porno magazines is not meditating.
65. Seek intensive psychotherapy.
66. Crying to a bartender is not psychotherapy.
67. Avoid swinging.
68. Avoid rat packing.
69. Avoid carousing.
70. Avoid canoodling.
71. What happens in Vegas stays in your colon.
72. Soak in a tub of warm glue.
73. (Sorry, I just wanted to see if you'd do it.)
74. Do clowns ever operate heavy machinery? Because...don't.
75. Some hopeless medical cases can be cured simply by laughter.
76. But not yours.
77. Stay awake.
78. Don't bother to eat.
79. Just sit there.
80. Take a bath tomorrow or the next day.
81. Six eye drops in each ear.
82. Six ear drops in each eye.
83. I know what I said. Just do it.
84. If nipples loosen, do not pull. (They will fall off on their own.)
85. Assemble a fellowship of young hearts brave and true.
86. Together find your way to the Mount of Doom.
87. Destroy the ring.
88. That rubber bag in the bathroom cabinet? With the tubes hanging out? I'm not going to say what it is. Just use it.
89. Avoid bending over.
90. If you must bend over, hold the palm of your hand firmly against your liver.
91. If your liver falls out anyway, consult a physician.
92. Not me.
93. Take five big-size swalleys o' corn likker and sleep it off in Granny Polecat's hidey-hole.
94. (Sorry, that last one was meant for Cletus Spuckler.)
95. If you hear an electronic beeping in your chest, remit any moneys owed to Dr. Julius Hibbert IMMEDIATELY!
96. You may feel scared, confused, or anxious about your medical condition. These feelings are abnormal. Do not share them with anyone.
97. Avoid song.
98. Avoid dance.
99. Avoid seltzer down your pants.
100. Always maintain a positive attitude.

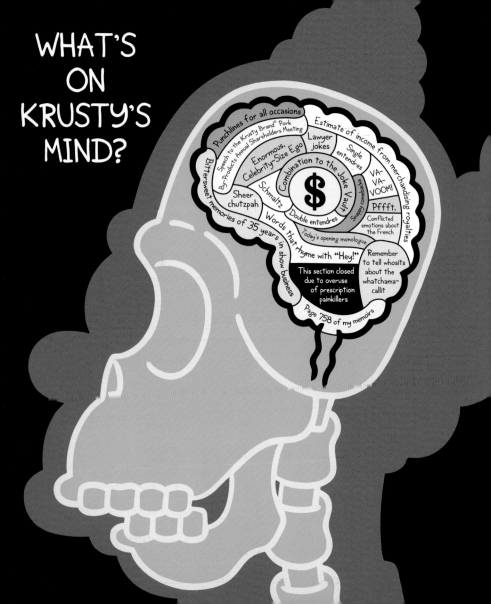

Li'L KRUSTY

KNOW YOUR KRUSTORY

with your host, Bart Simpson, Doctor of Krustology!

> IF **LOVE** IS THE BREAD OF LIFE, THEN **COMEDY** IS THE CEREAL, AND KRUSTY IS KING OF BOTH THE FUNNY **AND** THE FIBER! AND I'M NOT JUST TALKING ABOUT **KRUSTY O'S!** NO, KRUSTY HAS MADE A TON OF BREAKFAST FOOD IN HIS DAY. MONTH AFTER MONTH, YEAR AFTER YEAR, KRUSTY'S BEEN...

KEEPIN' IT CE-REAL!

Krusty's first food triumph came in the form of cereal. He found that forming cheap grain into shapes, packaging it in a colorful box with his face on it, and including a "special" plastic prize not only delivered a child's daily supply of sugar (and then some!) but also provided mouth-watering profit margins. Thus, throughout Krusty's career, he's always had at least one version of this staple in his merchandising stable...

Krusty O's™

remains the most popular Krusty breakfast experience. Oat husk remainders and spelt ends are pulverized, combined, mixed into synthetic molasses, and shaped lovingly into O's by a die press originally used to build tank lugnuts.

FREE FACE-PAINT INSIDE!

A LITTLE LECK OF UNLEAVENED HEAVEN!

Krusty Oy's™

is the popular, "Almost Kosher for Passover" version of Krusty O's™, available every spring.

Sideshow Mel's Shredded Wheat Hairbones™

was the short-lived cereal tribute to Krusty's sidekick, Sideshow Mel. Focus tests indicated that children wanted a cereal shaped like the fibia that holds Mel's hair up. It was later learned that this research was conducted with the participation of only "really crazy" children.

Krusty Crusts!™

is the cereal that's "the best part of the peanut butter and jelly sandwich—the crusts!" Unpopular with tot breakfasters and sold exclusively in discount stores, this cereal is often used by shepherds as cheap sheep feed.

Mallow K™

was marketed to adults. This product combined enriched marshmallows with nutrient-reduced chocolate. Mallo K™ was the first grainless cereal introduced to the U.S. market.

KrustyGel™

was called "the worst cereal debacle of the '80s." Billed as "The Tubular Cereal That Comes in a Tube!" KrustyGel™ was more of a paste than a cereal, composed of liquefied bulgar, dates, and fruit roll-up trimmings. Not only difficult to swallow and impossible to chew, the formulation of the cereal was rumored to cause sensitivity to sunlight and a "blue-ification of urine."

K-CREW CATALOG

Jorge—when I bought that warehouse full of mangy alpaca fur and faux chinchilla, my accountant called me delusional. Okay, maybe I was delusional from that week-old Chinese food and the absinthe, but you made a silk purse out of a sow's ear—literally! I LOVE that purse! And you also made those raw, garbagey materials I bought into grade-A yuppiewear! Bang up job, kiddo! Feel free to use the villa on Lake Springfield this weekend—you've earned it! (Just wash the dishes, strip the bed, and be out by six—it's a timeshare!)

— KRUSTY

(A) Krustyhair Trapper Cap™
More than 20 years of Krusty's barber sweepings have been made available for the production of this supple, traditional Trapper's Cap. The cap features a snap-up brim, Polywhatever™ lining, and little pockets for small bottles of booze. It's the cap early American settlers wore, but designed for today: sturdy, fashionable, and made of clown hair. S/M, M/L, FREAKISHLY L. **$525**

(B) Krusty Clown Nose Warmer™
Fashioned from recycled car seat vinyl and stuffed with warmifying packing foam, the Krusty Clown Nose Warmer keeps precious body heat from escaping your nose and keeps laughter in your heart. For people with rubber sensitivities, it could possibly provide a harmless*, mild tingling sensation in the outer extremities. S, M, L, DURANTE. **$45**

(C) Krusty Crushed Velvet Turquoise Bow Tie™
A loving reproduction of the tie Krusty wore on his legendary "Comeback Special." Untieable and worn loose to give the "I'm ready for drinkin'" look.
ONE SIZE FITS ALL (thick necks require two sewn together). **$50**

*mostly harmless

(A) Krusty Distressed Plastic Clown Shoes™
Pre-scuffed and broken in by obese Ukranian female factory workers, these replicas of Krusty's hilarious, heartwarming footwear are true to the original both inside and out. Moldings of Krusty's actual orthopedic inserts are included, as well as tiny, sound-encoded microchip speakers to mimic the sound of the cracking calcium deposits in Krusty's toe knuckles. Whole sizes 6–11M. (Persons with webbed toes are advised not to use this product.)

(B) Krusty Classic Remote-Activated Flapping Dickey™ **(with clown nose cufflink controls)**
The Krusty Flapping Dickey combines classic comedy and cutting-edge flapping technology. High-tension adamantium springs are woven into luxurious blanched cotton, then reinforced with teak tongue depressors. An infrared activated release is triggered by remote cufflinks featuring Krusty's nose. Egyptian felt lines the dickey's bottom, preventing accidental chin lacerations. Ivory buttons from genuine elephant tusks complete the garment, making it politically incorrect and, therefore, "edgy." Treat yourself with the prime rib of flapping dickeys by the man who claims to have invented them. Available only in XS, to heighten comic effect when worn by larger people.

(C) Krusty Trusty Hernia Truss™
The only commercially available hernia truss whimsically patterned with Krusty's face and with balanced protection for right, left, double, and even triple hernias. Includes adjustable padding and special medical-grade whoopee cushion built into seat. S, M, L, XL, XXL, WOWTHATSREALLY L.

SO YOU THINK ALL KRUSTY CARES ABOUT IS *KRUSTY*? WELL, GO JUMP IN THE *LAKE*, YOU LOUSY LITTLE *INGRATES*! I'VE GOT *COMPASSION* LEAKIN' OUT OF MY *EARS*! THAT'S MY PROBLEM! I'M *TOO GOOD*, AND THE WORLD IS *CRAWLING* WITH *DEADBEATS* BEGGING FOR A *HANDOUT* FROM ONE OF...

KRUSTY'S CHARITIES!

WOULD **YOU** WANT TO BE THE ONE TO TELL HIM?

BUY THE KID A BEER ALREADY!

March of Beers®

THERE'S NO BEER FOR *SPRING BREAK!*

BECAUSE $500,000,000,000 STRETCHES ONLY SO FAR

Krusty's 32nd Annual

WALKATHON FOR THE PENTAGON

HELP KRUSTY
RAISE MUCH-WANTED FUNDS FOR OUR HEROIC MILITARY BUREAUCRATS AND SELFLESS DEFENSE CONTRACTORS!

THESE CHILDREN ARE WAITING FOR A SCHOOL BUS THAT MIGHT NEVER COME

Unless Krusty's Back Taxes Are Paid

WON'T YOU HELP AMERICA RAISE TOMORROW'S LEADERS?

BUS STOP

KRUSTY THE CLOWN'S STAY OUT OF JAIL FOUNDATION
"Helping Others Eventually Since 1962"

CLOSE-UP

KRUSTY'S CRUSADE FOR THE CURE
(Telethon) 30 min.

"This is the last year I'm screwing around with this," announced Krusty the Clown between head-sized helpings of caviar at the 42nd Annual Crusade for the Cure launch party. "Nobody's getting better. It's just a depressing waste of time."

Krusty has quit his annual telethon more than a dozen times before—usually in disputes over hotel accommodations and expense accounts. If he means it this time, this may be your last chance to enjoy such recurring bits as "Stupid Convalescent Tricks," "Stump the Sick People," and the clown's tearful reunions with sworn enemies (this year: Joe Piscopo).

Highlights: None.

Li'L KRUSTY

Once upon a time there was a big, big comedy act called "The 3 Little Shnooks." Mind you, kids, I'm talking vaudeville — it's the only language I speak.

The 3 Little Shnooks headlined in every major theatre in the country. Not just the Borsht circuit. Big cities: New York, Chicago, Philly, Capital City. They were the top of the heap. The cream of the crop. They were bigger than Al Jolson, Sophie Tucker, and Fanny Brice put together. What do you mean, "Who were they?" You think you little pishers invented big name entertainment?

Anyhow, this act killed. No kidding. People came from all over to see The 3 Little Shnooks do their shtick. Variety called it "a funsational mirthquake!" They had 'em rolling in the aisles. These guys practically invented slapstick: the *pie-in-the-face*, the *double take*, the *seltzer spritz*. The whole magilla.

The 3 Little Shnooks were beloved by all. Dames threw themselves at their feet. Men bought them drinks and slapped them on the back. They were wined and dined by presidents and kings. What more could three shmoes from Springfield's Lower East Side ask for? They had it all, kids. Fame. Fortune.

Ah, but Fame she is a fickle mistress. A real psycho, that Fame. And Fortune is a bit of a nut job, too, I'll tell you. Hoo boy! A pair of Jezebels, the both of them. They build you up and then Kaboom! They knock you down. They plant little seeds of doubt from which grow a boundless field of discontented weeds.

And that's what happened to The 3 Little Shnooks. At the very height of their fame they looked into each other's eyes, and all that each Little Shnook could see was his own reflected glory. Each Little Shnook thought that without him the act was nothing. Zilch. Zero. Zip. And so each Little Shnook decided to leave the act and go solo. Stop me if you've heard this one before, kids.

So, the first Little Shnook puts together a boffo, socko single act with some song, some dance, and a pair of baggy pants. Tickets sell like hotcakes. It's standing room only. He's packing 'em in! But he ain't wowing 'em, you know what I mean? They ain't booing the Little Shnook, but they ain't yukking it up, either. He's gone tepid, kids, which means he ain't so hot.

Then the second Little Shnook goes solo with a sure-fire routine. Plenty of jokes, lots of laughs, he even has a line of chorus girls that shake a mean hootchie-cootchie, you should pardon the expression. It's the season's hot ticket. It can't miss! But it does. Not by a mile, but it misses. It ain't quite a turkey, but it still lays an egg.

Now it's the third Little Shnook's turn in the spotlight. I'll spare you the details, kids; suffice it to say he stunk up Broadway. Both sides of the street.

See what I mean, kids? Kaboom! The biggest act in show business was reduced to just three little gigs. They quickly went from ho-hum to p-u. From riches to rags, spiraling downward to the bottom of the bill. Three lousy singles playing third-rate burlesque houses. Soon even the hicks in the sticks were saying nix to their tricks.

Until one night when they found themselves booked on the same bill at the Springfield Bawdy-Ville Theatre.

Three Little Shnooks in the basement of their careers. They looked into each other's eyes and each Little Shnook could see the dim reflection of his own glorious past.

Each Little Shnook realized that without the other two, he was nothing. Nada. Squat. Bubkes.

Before you could say Bob's your uncle, they checked their egos at the door, got their original act back together, and took their show out on the road. Hey, hey, hey! The 3 Little Shnooks were back, baby! Wow-zah! Wow-zah! And so they spent the rest of their lives doing the same shtick in one-night stands at progressively smaller and smaller theatres until, one by one, they each did their ultimate solo turn—dying broke and alone in some fleabag hotel off Times Square.

That's showbiz, kids. You're up, you're down, you're in, you're out. Friday you're hot-cha-cha, by Monday you're cold as leftover mashed potatoes. Top banana one day, next day you're playing the horses' patootie in some burley-que show. Which reminds me of the story about Goldie Lox and the Three Blintzes…Ah, maybe some other time.

Li'L KRUSTY

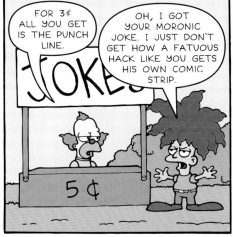

Descended from a long line of rabbis, Krusty the Clown's father, Rabbi Hyman Krustofski, is one of the most respected men on the lower east side of Springfield. People come from miles around to ask his advice, while others call the KBBL radio show "Gabbin' about God," which he cohosts with Reverend Timothy Lovejoy and Monsignor Kenneth Daley. His 25-year estrangement from his son Herschel (a.k.a. Krusty) ended after an epiphany brought on by the immortal words of Sammy Davis, Jr.

- **Quote:** "Life is not fun; life is serious. Seltzer is for drinking, not for spraying. Pie is for noshing, not for throwing."

- **Dress:** Orthodox.
- **Speech:** Rapid and upward inflected.
- **Manner:** Stubborn.
- **Favorite pastimes:** Chess, Yahtzee, and answering questions with questions.
- **Likes:** Saul Bellow, steam baths, and a nice sandwich.
- **Dislikes:** Fatty meats, sauerkraut, and the filmed ouevre of Bruce Willis.
- **Selected reference books:** "The Big Book of Chosen People," "Views on Jews," "Jewishness Revisited," and "Yes I Can" by Sammy Davis, Jr.
- **His sage advice:** "The best charity is to give and not let other people know;" "No one is poor, except he who lacks knowledge;" and "Great is the car with power steering and Dyna-Flow suspension."
- **Among his famous midrashes:** "Coping with Christians," "What's So Funny about Clowns?" and "Did Not a Wise Man Once Say..."
- **Krusty's reconciliation music:** "Oh, Mein Papa," with instrumental accompaniment by The Krums.

I THINK ABOUT MY FATHER ALL THE TIME EXCEPT WHEN I'M AT THE TRACK. THEN IT'S ALL BUSINESS.

SOPHIE KRUSTY'S LONG LOST ILLEGITIMATE DAUGHTER

To find her dad, Sophie types "pathetic clown" into a search engine, and after retrieving Krusty's name, she tracks him down at the Springfield Festival of Books, where he is doing a signing. Sophie's innocence and sweetness soften Krusty's heart to the point that when he loses her violin in a poker game he actually risks his life to get it back.

- **Quote:** "You know, for a clown, you're not really a lot of fun."

- **Genetic inheritance:** Green hair and musical talent—which skips generations, just like diabetes.
- **Cute distinguishing marks:** Symmetrical freckles.
- **Dress:** White shirt, blue skirt, purple vest, and shoes.
- **Krusty's first reaction to Sophie:** "I think I just seltzered myself."
- **Favorite beach activities:** Throwing the Frisbee, running from waves, boogie boarding, fishing, enjoying the sunset, and eating ice cream while riding a surfing horse.
- **Violin appraisal:** Won't bring much cash, but its sentimental value is through the roof.
- **Krusty's affectionate term of endearment:** My Little Hamentashen.

I'M NOT THE KIND OF DAD WHO, YOU KNOW, DOES THINGS, OR SAYS STUFF, OR LOOKS AT YOU. BUT THE LOVE IS THERE.

While entertaining the troops during the Gulf War, Krusty is forced to take shelter during a desert storm where he meets Sophie's mom. Dressed in low-cut camouflage pants and a crop top, she and Krusty entertain each other all night. Consequently, when back in the States, she truthfully explains that Sophie's father is "some pathetic clown."

- **Quote:** "Grrrrrrrrr."

- **Description:** Chestnut brown hair, kind of shy, thirty-two confirmed kills.
- **Krusty's romantic reverie:** "There was your mother, lookin' like a beautiful mirage. Maybe it was the anthrax in the air. Maybe it was the fact the Arab women weren't bitin'. Whatever it was, it was magic."
- **Her secret mission:** To assassinate Saddam Hussein.
- **Her weapon:** Handheld surface-to-air missile.
- **Her plan:** Thwarted by Krusty.
- **Her wheels:** Chevy Impala.
- **Her current dress:** Pantsuits.
- **Her current demeanor:** Barely suppressed rage.
- **Her fabulous clown art collection:** Four paintings: Three clowns dangling by their necks from nooses; the head of a clown melting in Hell; a decapitated clown, seated; and a clown being violently executed in an electric chair. Two sculptures: one clown with an axe buried in its head and another with a knife in the back.

WHAT CAN I SAY? WHEN YOU'RE IN A WAR ZONE YOU DON'T WANT TO BE FIRING BLANKS.

To avoid punishment for massive tax fraud or as Kent Brockman would say "tax avoision," Krusty the Clown fakes his own death in a fiery plane crash, then takes on the identity of Rory B. Bellows, an itinerant beach-comber, lobster fisherman, and sea-faring handyman. Through the persona of Rory, Krusty momentarily discovers his true calling in life: salvaging sunken barges for scrap iron.

- **Quote:** "Who needs friends? The incessant beep of the global positioning system is all the companionship I need."

- **Dress:** White wife-beater, blue jeans, and light blue deck shoes.
- **Drives:** Reddish brown pick-up truck.
- **Disguise:** Brushy brown mustache and goatee, and fake yellow nose.
- **Telltale Rory/Krusty similarities:** Pacemaker scar, identical signature, and superfluous third nipple.
- **Favorite pastimes:** Trolling for tuna, getting seasick, and bouncing checks at The Sea Cap'n's Bait 'n' Barg'n B'n.
- **Benefits of ocean living:** The sea air cleans your lungs, the sun toasts pale skin a healthy brown, and the ocean provides a vast bounty of mercury-laden food.
- **Drawbacks of ocean living:** The merry sounds of Handsome Pete's relentless sea chanteys.
- **Plane used to fake death:** The "I'm On-A-Rolla Gay."
- **Krusty's upbeat tombstone farewell:** "See ya real soon kids!"

NEXT TO ME, HE'S THE HANDSOMEST GUY I KNOW.

KNOW YOUR KRUSTORY
with your host, Bart Simpson, Doctor of Krustology!

OKAY, LET'S ADMIT IT. THE MAN HAS MADE SOME MISTAKES. THERE WAS THE KRUSTY EXPLODING NUTCRACKER™. THE KRUSTY ALLIGATOR WRESTLING FEDERATION. THE TIME HE ATE INDIAN FOOD FROM A TRUCK RIGHT BEFORE A TRANS-ATLANTIC FLIGHT. BUT NONE OF THESE MISSTEPS HAS BEEN AS PERMANENT, AS ETERNAL, OR AS STAINED-ON-CELLULOID AS...

The Film Flops
of Krusty the Clown!

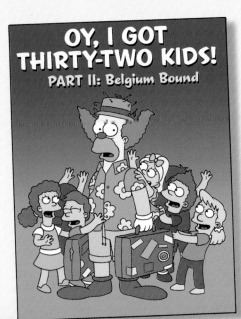

PLOT FORMULA
(Krusty + Orphans)2 + Belgium = Hilarious. Twice.

WORLDWIDE GROSS
$234,137

NOTABLE REVIEW
"This sequel to the previous film about a down-on-his-luck clown who inherits a mustard factory along with nearly three dozen orphans DID NOT NEED TO BE MADE!"
—Anthony Devereaux, *Gilly Parish News*

The original film did surprisingly "not terrible" box office. Thus, Krusty immediately embarked on a hastily produced follow-up. Plunging forward without a script, the only financing he could find was from the Belgian government. Needless to say, a wine-drunk, chocolate-bloated Krusty, improvising with confused children in the city of Antwerp, did not add up to hilarity.

PLOT FORMULA
(Krusty x '90s Hip-Hop) +
bikini girls + beer + "borrowed"
yacht + donkey in a cowboy hat =
Laugh Out Loud Funny.

WORLDWIDE GROSS
18 million kroon (Estonian currency)

NOTABLE REVIEW
"Hip-Hop away from this
film as quickly as possible...
by land, sea, or air."
—Mr. MovieHead,
San Jose Action 14 News

Made as an "homage"
(read: rip off) to *House Party 2:
Pajama Jammy Jam*, this film
implausibly features Krusty
as the president of a fraternity,
trying to save the Kappa Lambda
Omega frathouse by holding a
"flickysmicky on the sea."
No one knew what a
"flickysmicky" was or, for
that matter, any of the other
sixty-three words Krusty made up
and copyrighted as "Krusty Slang."

Booty Cruise!

KRUSTY ALMIGHTY!

PLOT FORMULA
Krusty + The Father + The Son + The Holy Ghost = Box Office Heaven.

WORLDWIDE GROSS
-$14 million

NOTABLE FACT
The film's proceeds went to a faith-based organization serving destitute clowns. (Krusty was unaware of this when he signed on to do the film.)

NOTABLE REVIEW
"I found myself praying for this film to end."
—G.L. Laneton, *Westfield News Intelligencer*

In *Krusty Almighty!* Krusty tried his hand at Christian entertainment—with predictably bad results. The unbelievable plot featured Krusty playing a clown-in-crisis, trying to find meaning by becoming a priest. It didn't work. One critic, Charlotte Imbimburg of *The Torrance Caunan Clippers Weekly Circular*, stated plainly, "After seeing this film, I've come to a conclusion: THERE IS NO GOD." Krusty's extravagant expenditures during the shoot (including luxurious private trailers for his barber, masseuse, and bookie, as well as imported kimodo dragon steak dinners) actually drew money away from the charity, closing it down. As a result, clown homeless-ness has gone up 112% since the film's release.

PLOT FORMULA
(Krusty x Blue Collar Shmoe) +
winning lottery ticket =
Relatable Everyday Fantasy and
Boffo Box Office.

WORLDWIDE GROSS
$67,289 (one time showing on
The Lottery Channel)

LOGLINE
"You Win Some, You Lose
Your Mind."

NOTABLE REVIEW
"Okay, let me save you
eighty minutes of your life.
Krusty plays Otto, a guy who
gets a lottery ticket from his
pals on his birthday.
He wins, they want a cut,
and he says, "Sorry, loserinos,
these simoleons are MINE!"
twenty-eight times.
And there's a song by Rush."
—Shelley Piersons, *Soybean
Growers News and Lifestylo*

Krusty edged out
Kevin James for the
role of Otto. On the night
of the premiere, Kevin James
was heard to remark,
"My god, I really dodged
a bullet there."

JERK WIN$ LOTTO

KRUSTY ENTERTAINS OUR TROOPS

An Excerpt from: THE GROOVIEST GENERATION
By Channel 6 News Anchor Kent Brockman

When this reporter thinks of war, he thinks of—that is, I think of—laughter. Laughter and, yes, fun and games, thanks to the antics of a happy clown named Krusty. I was working in a Swiss girls boarding school during the war of my youth, which raged, I believe, somewhere in Asia. The only way I got to experience the excitement was through nightly news programming like "SwissWatch Action News at 5:30 with Ulrich Euler." These broadcasts were primitive predecessors to the ones I anchor weeknights at 5:00 and 11:00 on Springfield's Channel 6, which is Channel 7 on SpringCast Cable and Channel 129 in Hi-Def. (And don't forget my weekly podcast, downloadable from my blog, KentTouchThis! at http://springfieldlibraryweb.gov/users/suspended/overduematerials/kenttouchthisblog/kentbrockmp3.htm.)

So, back to Krusty. I saw the footage on "SwissWatch Action News" the night before he shipped out to bring our troops the brand of laughter only seltzer and big shoes can supply. I wept with anchor Ulrich Euler as he reflected on the courage of Krusty, explaining that, in war, even a clown could get hurt. I wondered then if Krusty knew that. I forgot all about the brave and bold clown, until news broke of his midnight arrest and subsequent military tribunal. The charge: TREASON.

The Pentagon proved that Krusty had built his act around the Army's future troop movements. He would use dancers, acrobats, tumblers, code words, and drawings in the sand to divulge America's secret plans. He claimed it was a tribute. But the court sentenced Krusty the Clown to death.

What saved him? His own crafty clownish cunning and, clearly, cowardice. It seems Krusty knew full well Ulrich Euler's admonition that, in war, even a clown could get hurt. So he secretly stayed home, laying low while a paid ringer in greasepaint went on the tour and took all the harrowing risks for him. And also spied.

When the real story broke, Krusty was exonerated and a relieved nation laughed. And we laughed again a month later when the Army executed the spy.

KRUSTYBROOK
❧ Woods ☙

You've made some money. You've had some kids. Now, you need a home. But settling down doesn't have to mean settling for *less*. In fact, it could mean laughs, zaniness, and hilarity… for the rest of your life!

Krustybrook Woods is a modern planned community that combines a picturesque country setting, finely fabricated homes, and charm up the wazoo. It's a place that's lousy with novelty topiaries, homes with downspouts, and plenty of hilarious covenants, conditions, and restrictions.

THE HOMES

- All Krustybrook Woods homes feature "comedy enhancing" amenities, such as dumbwaiters, extra-springy clotheslines, built-in ironing boards, and extra-slick banisters.
- Kitchens come complete with giant chef's hats, recipes for collapsing soufflés, hilarious aprons, novelty straws, and banana peel compatible tiling.

THE SURROUNDINGS

- The forest surrounding Krustybrook Woods has been stocked with funny animals like titmice, howler monkeys, and cuckoos.
- There's fresh air, and there's *fresh* air. Krustybrook Woods is a fully scented community—residents of the development can look forward to days filled with Grin™, Krusty's signature perfume, sprayed over Krustybrook Woods daily by crop-dusting planes painted to look like Krusty's head.

THE LOCATION

Springfield is an incredible city-town with beaches, mountains, deserts, rainforests, glens, bogs, malls, bars, and twenty-seven Krusty Burger™ outlets. Add to that a school system that has been deemed "adequate" twice in the past five years, roads that feature working stoplights, and a police force that owns a helicopter, and you come up with a location equation that equals home! That being said, residents can return to the safety of Krustybrook Woods where they will be surrounded and protected by its twelve-foot security wall and Israeli-trained security force.

So Come Home to Krustybrook Woods Where the Livin' is Krusty!

Home | Browse | Search | Invite | Film | Mail | Blog | Favorites

KOSHER KOMEDY KING

"For those about to laff, I salute you."

Male
Springfield
USA

View My: Pics | Videos

Last Login:
10 minutes ago

Krusty's Interests

General
Cigars, bourbon, cigarettes, vodka, dames, broads, the ponies, hangin' with chimps, pie-based comedy, merchandising up the wazoo, pork products, tiny bicycle tricks, golf

Music
Don Johnson, Eddie Murphy, David Hasselhoff, Bruce Willis, Scott Baio, Shaquille O'Neal, Joey Lawrence, the Bacon Brothers

Movies
The Day the Clown Cried, The Jazz Singer (Neil Diamond version), *Mr. Saturday Night, Big Top Pee-Wee*, anything with Buddy Hackett

Television
Horse racing simulcasts, KrustyTrim™ infomercials, anything with Nancy Dussault, that show with the cops

Books
Yes, I Can by Sammy Davis, Jr.
(the audiobook version as read by Michael York)

Heroes
My dad, Johnny Carson, Yakov Smirnoff, Billy Crystal, Gandhi

Krusty's Friends

 CultureClubber

 RollerChimp

 BardLover64

 PonyGal

 I.P. Freely

 Li'lHamentashen

 GymBag

THE IMPROBABLE THINKINGS OF A KOSHER KOMEDY KING:
THE OFFICIAL BLOG OF KRUSTY THE CLOWN

August 3
ld6ig degtgisvit gtgidvghldyyglidyl ygpu0u7gty6i8 7igfydfgyiu. Oy. Keyboard was upside down and covered with gravy.

September 22
Last night was a wild one. Me and Mr. Teeny tied one on, snuck into the Springfield Zoo, and swam with the penguins. I woke up next to a walrus. Teeny was missing. After doing my business behind a meshuganah ice cap, I went looking for my monkey. The zookeeper told me they found a loose chimp and tossed him back in the ape house. All monkeys without fezzes and bow ties look the same to me. Good thing he was still wearing his roller skates.

November 2
I just ate the thickest, grilled cheese sandwich ever made. Five inches high with six types of cheeses. Man, that's livin'.

November 6
Laid up for the last three days. Turns out I'm lactose intolerant. Too much cheese put me in a world of hurt. Who knew?

December 3
You know what gets me? The way the IRS says "we're sorry to inconvenience you" in their audit letters now. Hey, if you don't want to inconvenience me, DON'T THREATEN TO SEIZE MY LLAMA RANCH!

December 11
Springfield is a lousy town for knishes.

December 12
I can't type. I hired a kid to do it, but it turns out he can't type either. So his sister is on the keys; she's a egghead. (Typist's note: My name is Lisa Simpson, and I don't like to be called "a egghead." First, it's "an egghead," and second, I am not one.)

February 1
I don't do Botox because it helps my poker game, but I don't not do it because it helps my poker game, either.

February 8
Oh, god. I just ate a ton of Silly Putty. I thought it was some crazy new kind of egg. This is bad. I'm all gummed up.

Li'L KRUSTY

ANATOMY OF KRUSTY

1. **Hair** – Green as the day he was born.
2. **Face** – Showbiz is in his blood—literally. (Clown White makeup courses through his veins after years of constant use.)
3. **Seltzer Bottle** – One time: comedic squirt; three times: clownish flirt!
4. **Cream Pie** – He's never met a cream pie that he didn't throw.
5. **Ball** – It takes balls to juggle on live TV!

"Krusty's Animal Pals" segment of show (which inspired new segment, "Visit From Dr. Tetanus Shot").

12. **Shoes** – He may wear big floppies, but he's got tiny feet, like all good-hearted people.
13. **Sideshow What's-his-name** – devoted sidekick.
14. **Animal Mascot** – Loyal, humble, incredibly stinky—and it's not just the stogie.
15. **Stomach** – Home of vulgar appetites, such as condor egg omelets and spotted owl soup.
16. **Superfluous Third Nipple** – Always good for a laugh and for scaring girls at parties.
17. **Elbow** – Inspiration for Krusty's new plush toy: Tickle Me, Elbow.
18. **Spinning Bow Tie** – Great gag when it works; crippling neck pain when it doesn't.
19. **Wrist** – Suffers from Carnival Tunnel Syndrome.
20. **Cigarette** – There's nothing better than a cigarette lit with a hundred-dollar bill.

6. **Nasal Prophylactic** – Good for keeping out the smell of Kent Brockman's fancy-ass cheeses.
7. **Gloves** – Traditional harlequin wear since classic Italian Commedia Dell'Arte (great for hiding nicotine stains, fingerprints, and prison tattoos).
8. **Heart** – Needs a pacemaker (caused by and paid for by Krusty Brand Pork® Products).
9. **Ribs** – Funny bones!
10. **Pocket** – Contains a copy of the audio book "Steal These Humorous Quips" by Steve Allen.
11. **Legs** – Concentration of scars from

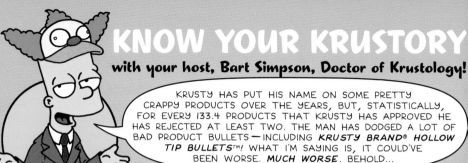

KNOW YOUR KRUSTORY

with your host, Bart Simpson, Doctor of Krustology!

KRUSTY HAS PUT HIS NAME ON SOME PRETTY CRAPPY PRODUCTS OVER THE YEARS, BUT, STATISTICALLY, FOR EVERY 133.4 PRODUCTS THAT KRUSTY HAS APPROVED HE HAS REJECTED AT LEAST TWO. THE MAN HAS DODGED A LOT OF BAD PRODUCT BULLETS—INCLUDING *KRUSTY BRAND® HOLLOW TIP BULLETS*™! WHAT I'M SAYING IS, IT COULD'VE BEEN WORSE. *MUCH WORSE*. BEHOLD...

THE PRODUCTS THAT DIDN'T MAKE THE KRUSTY CUT!

H & R Krusty's
Home Tax Evasion Kit™

Cuzzin' Krusty's Moonshine Still™

Dr. Krusty's
Home Mole Removal Kit™

KrustyPetz®
Dog Taunter

Krusty's
Individually-Wrapped
Pudding Skins™

Uncle Krusty's
Termite Farm™

KrustyKare® Eterno-Rest Caskets and Headstones

Krustofski Home Gefilte Fish Kit™
(includes: three carp, aquarium, fish food, scaler, gutting knife, and fish meat grinder)

Krusty's Clown Car Smell Aerosol Spray™

The Krusty Holiday Ham Bust™
(a lovingly rendered likeness of Krusty in molded pork)

Cap'n Krusty's Slow-Aged Fishing Chum™

Herschel the Hippie Brand® Organic Horse Glue

KrustySmooth® X-tra Strength Stool Softening Bubble Gum

Krusty's U.S. Quarter-Sized Metal Slugs™

Not pictured:
• The Krusty Home Botulism Cosmetic Injection Kit™
• KrustyFarms® Industrial Veal Pen
• KrustyFem® Sanitary Napkins (with wings in the shape of Krusty's signature clown haircut)

KRUSTY'S MAILBOX

Dear Krusty,

I am eight years old. I watch your show every day on Channel 6, and I scream and cry and make my mommy buy all your Krusty Brand toys and cereals just like you tell me to. Some of my little friends say that there is no Krusty the Clown. They say it's just some baldheaded jackass in green pants. Papa says, "If Kent Brockman says it on 'Springfield Action News,' it's so." Well, I'd sooner eat my body weight in Brussels sprouts than watch one minute of Kent Brockman…so, please tell me the truth, is there really a Krusty the Clown?

Virginia O'Hanrahan

Dear Krusty,

I will not subject my precious child to another day of "fun" at Kamp Krusty, and I, hereby, demand a full refund of my ex-husband's money. You are a menace to summer, Krusty. Have you no sense of decency left, sir, at long last? Have you left no sense of decency?

Luanne Van Houten
Divorcée

Dear Krusty,

I just love your show! I am a nine-year-old girl with green hair and tiny feet and frequent cravings for pork products. My question to you is: did you by any chance pass through Peoria years ago?

Signed,
Puzzled in Peoria

Springfield City Court House
RESTRAINING ORDER

Melvin Van Horne, AKA Sideshow Mel [Plaintiff] Vs.
Mr. Herschel Krustofski, AKA Krusty the Clown [Defendant]

It is hereby ordered that the defendant, Mr. Herschel Krustofski, AKA Krusty the Clown, is temporarily enjoined from:

1. Coming within 500 yards or within cream pie-throwing distance of Melvin Van Horne, AKA Sideshow Mel.

2. Additionally, you are prohibited from employing any and all cigar-smoking chimpanzees as proxy throwers of said cream pies.

3. Additionally, you are hereby ordered to refrain from the use of butane, propane, or any type of natural or synthetic gas-powered blowtorches in your comedy routine.

Dear Krusty,

Please find enclosed $2,568.39 for the home version of Krusty's Iron Lung. I can hardly wait 'til it arrives. SERIOUSLY.

Your pal,
Little Timmy

To: Virginia O'Hanrahan

Yes, Virginia, there is a Krusty the Clown. He exists as certainly as Krusty Brand® Imitation Gruel, Krusty-O's™ cereal, Krusty's Home Pregnancy Test™, Krusty Non-Narkotik Kough Syrup™, Krusty mugs and T-shirts exist–and you know that all those products abound and give to your life its highest beauty and joy.

Alas! How dreary would be the world if there were no Krusty the Clown! It would be as dreary as if there were no Virginias. Not believe in Krusty the Clown! You might as well not believe in fairies or elves or executive assistants.

Ah, Virginia, Krusty the Clown lives and lives forever. A thousand years from now, Virginia, nay 10 times 10,000 years from now, his estate will continue to make a percentage on goods targeted at the very heart of childhood.

Sincerely,

Miss Lois Pennycandy,
Executive Assistant to Krusty the Clown

cc:ktc

Dear Krusty,

This is Bart Simpson, Krusty Buddy #16302, respectfully returning his badge. I always suspected that nothing in life mattered. Now I know for sure.

Get Bent,
Bart Simpson

CEASE & DESIST NOTICE

Recipient: Mr. Herschel Krustofski, AKA Krusty the Clown
Re: The Bob Hope Estate vs. The Comedic Stylings of Krusty the Clown

We have recently learned that you have acquired various jokes from the Bob Hope Estate and have incorporated this material in your alleged comedy act.

As you are no doubt, aware, Bob Hope's legacy to the world is his beloved humor. Your boorish, ham-fisted attempt to alter Mr. Hope's material to suit your so-called comedic routine is a direct infringement on this legacy as well as a repugnant blotch on the entire entertainment profession.

We, hereby, demand that you confirm to us in writing within ten (10) days of receipt of this letter that: (I) you have removed all infringing materials from your wretched repertoire; and (II) you will refrain from inflicting any similar routines on any members of the public in the future.

The foregoing is without waiver of any and all rights of the Bob Hope Estate, all of which are expressly reserved herein.

Very truly yours,
Sheldon J. Fenderstone, esq.
Attorney-at-Law

Krusty's Scrapbook:
The Las Vegas Years

In 1962, I was approached by top businessman Murdering Mort "The Murderer" Murderosi (3rd from left) to do 1,000 shows at his casino, Nero's Trough. Once Mr. Murderosi explained the deal, this clown didn't need any convincing!

Was I a big deal in this town? Hey, I was the only entertainer in Vegas history to get my own slot machine on stage! And it paid off sometimes, too! Nothin' beats hittin' the jackpot in front of an audience full of losers!

Yeah, I loved that slot machine.

COPS CHASE CLOWN
Situation Not As Funny As It Sounds

But all good things must come to an end, and so I left swingin' Vegas for swingin' Branson, Missouri.

You gotta be willing to change in this business... or you're DEAD!

LISTEN, KIDS! DON'T EVER GROW UP TO BE FAMOUS LIKE *ME!* EVERYBODY WANTS A *PIECE* OF YA! "OH, KRUSTY, *PLEASE* DONATE TO THE HURRICANE VICTIMS!" "OH, KRUSTY, PAY OFF YOUR *HORSE BETS*, OR WE'LL BREAK YOUR *LEGS!*" "OH, KRUSTY, *I'M* YOUR LONG-LOST LITTLE *DAUGHTER! LOVE* ME!" IT'S ENOUGH TO MAKE YA *PLOTZ!*

BUT THE WORST OF *ALL* ARE THE *PAPARAZZI* (PAP-AH-*ROT*-SEE)! THESE SNEAKY, BLOODSUCKING LEECHES LURK IN FILTHY DUMPSTERS AND SMELLY TOILET STALLS WITH THEIR CHEAP IMPORTED CAMERAS, HOPING TO SNAP UGLY PICTURES OF *BIG STARS* LIKE *ME! T*HEN THEY SELL 'EM TO SCUMMY TABLOIDS FOR A KING'S RANSOM...AND *I* DON'T GET A *NICKEL!* SO, IN THE NAME OF MY MONEY, PLEASE, PLEASE, *PLEASE*, DON'T LOOK AT THESE...

CANDID PAPARAZZI PIX OF KRUSTY!

COVER:
I'M MOVING!

INTERIOR:
THANKS FOR NOT NOTICING I'VE BEEN STEALING YOUR WIFI CONNECTION.

COVER:
SORRY I SAID THAT INSENSITIVE THING ABOUT (FILL IN ETHNIC GROUP).

INTERIOR:
I DIDN'T KNOW YOUR MOTHER/FATHER WAS A (FILL IN ETHNIC GROUP).

COVER:
MOM AND DAD, SORRY I'M FAILING OUT OF SCHOOL.

INTERIOR:
HEY, AT LEAST I DIDN'T CHEAT!

COVER:
I SINCERELY WISH THIS CARD HAD BEEN PRINTED ON RECYCLED PAPER.

INTERIOR:
HAPPY EARTH DAY!

COVER:
HAPPY NATIONAL KRUSTY DAY!

INTERIOR:
SEND HIM MONEY IN THIS PRE-ADDRESSED ENVELOPE!

COVER:
OKAY, OKAY, OKAY! I'M SORRY I LEFT YOU AT THE ALTAR!

INTERIOR:
WILL YOU JUST SHUT UP ABOUT IT?

COVER:
ALL THINGS MUST PASS...

INTERIOR:
...ESPECIALLY YOUR KIDNEY STONE.

COVER:
IT'S A DOG EAT DOG WORLD...

INTERIOR:
...SO IT'S PRETTY WEIRD THAT MY DOG ATE YOUR CAT. SORRY ABOUT THAT.

COVER:
SORRY ABOUT YOUR FISH.

INTERIOR:
BUT I'D SAY WE'RE BOTH AT FAULT: YOU SHOULDN'T HAVE ASKED ME TO FEED IT, AND I SHOULD HAVE FED IT.

COVER:
YOU PARK GREAT!

INTERIOR:
I'M BEING SARCASTIC, DIPWAD.

Li'L KRUSTY

GABBO & ARTHUR CRANDALL KIDDIE-SHOW DUMMY AND VENTRILOQUIST

With a high-profile advertising blitz and a shameless no-holds-barred musical extravaganza, "The Gabbo Show" is introduced to Springfield, competing directly with "The Krusty the Clown Show" at 4:00 P.M. Gabbo's catch phrase "I'm a bad widdle boy" sweeps through town like a virus, threatening Krusty's livelihood. "The Gabbo Show" not only successfully steals Itchy & Scratchy from Krusty, it also steals his jokes, his bits, his audience, and, finally, his self-respect.

- **Quote:** Gabbo: "That oughta hold the little SOBs."
  Arthur Crandall: "Gabbo...quiet."

- **Gabbo's identifying characteristics:** Red hair, symmetrical freckles, huge over-bite, googly eyes, little bowler hat, light blue suit, red tie and cummerbund, and black shoes with spats.
- **Arthur Crandall's identifying characteristics:** Urbane, sophisticated, slicked-back hair, pencil mustache, red bow tie and cummerbund, and black tuxedo.
- **Gabbo's special skills:** Can do the Hully Gully, imitate Vin Scully, and travel back in time.
- **Arthur Crandall's special skill:** Can smoke and ventriloquize simultaneously.
- **Transportation:** A silver Bentley.
- **The Gabbo Puppet Players:** English guardsmen with rifles and busbies, Russian cossack dancers, juggling clowns, musical jesters, and French Can-Can girls.
- **Gabbo products and services:** Gabbo dolls, Gabbo doorstops, Gabbo Brand® Air Freshener, Gabbo's Guide to Gargling, and Gabbo Airlines.
- **Other TV competitors:** Bumblebee Man on Channel Ocho.
- **Krusty's counter-programming:** Eastern Europe's favorite cat-and-mouse team, Worker & Parasite.

> BAH, THAT DUMMY DOESN'T SCARE ME. I'VE HAD PLENTY OF GUYS COME AFTER ME. HOBOS, SEA CAPTAINS, JOEY BISHOP...AND I'VE BURIED THEM ALL!

A network executive who loves networking, Lindsey Naegle is a determined go-getter with scads of zazz whose number one concern is looking out for number one by filling her bank account with lots of mazuma. Her relentlessly vacuous notes championing both sides of any issue let her take credit for success while avoiding blame for failure. She urges Krusty to be dangerous, but warm, and edgy cute. She also advises him to open it up, run wild, shatter boundaries, slash-and-burn—without alienating anyone.

- **Quote:** "You can kill me, but two more will take my place."

- **Hair:** Upswept and dynamic.
- **Dress:** Skirt suits worn well north of the knee.
- **Demeanor:** Perky, pert, and predatory.
- **Hobbies:** Spouting platitudes, dancing to '80s power pop, and drinking.
- **Affiliations:** Member of the Springfield Chapter of Mensa, featured guest at the Springfield Speakers Bureau, and group facilitator at Alcoholics Anonymous.
- **Innovations:** The "Godcam" a jumbo-tron of faith-based fun, selling ad space in churches, and giving notes during live TV broadcasts.
- **Related job history:** Advanced Capital Ventures, creating synergy and books on how to cheat at bridge; rebranding the First Church of Springfield; customer service rep at Zovuvazz Phone Company (formerly Comquaaq); television producer of "The Afternoon Yak"; product positioning research for Kids First Industries (makers of Funzo™); and market research for Itchy & Scratchy International.

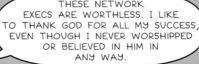

THESE NETWORK EXECS ARE WORTHLESS. I LIKE TO THANK GOD FOR ALL MY SUCCESS, EVEN THOUGH I NEVER WORSHIPED OR BELIEVED IN HIM IN ANY WAY.

FAT TONY LEGITIMATE BUSINESSMAN

William "Fat Tony" D'Amico (a.k.a. William "Fat Tony" Williams) is a high ranking associate in the DiMaggio organization headed up by Don Vittorio. Fat Tony is skilled in the art of gentle persuasion and turns to violence only as a last resort—or for the laughs. Whatever else you might say about Fat Tony, he is gracious. His itemized extortion bills always include a smiley face, and if overnight guests need money laundered, they can just set it outside their door and then pick it up the next morning.

- **Quote:** "Okay, Krusty, we will let the bet ride, but only because you crack us so consistently...up."

- **Real name:** Marion.
- **Website address:** crime.org
- **Rival crime families:** The Cuomos, Travoltas, Lasordas, and Boyardees.
- **Likes:** Expensive cigars, dark suits, and small bills—unmarked and nonsequential.
- **Dislikes:** Rotten squealers, tasteless Manhattans, and pasta sauce from a can.
- **Peculiar habit:** When he cries, he dabs his eyes with a slice of pizza.
- **Mode of transportation:** Touring car with a hood ornament shaped like an Emmy®.
- **Dream jobs deferred:** Pizza man, organ grinder, or leaning tower maker.
- **Special skills:** Virtuoso violin playing, imitating Marlon Brando, and making criminal acts seem philanthropic.

WHEN IT COMES TO COLLECTING DEBTS, FAT TONY SHOWED ME I WAS WRONG. YOU *CAN* SQUEEZE BLOOD OUT OF A TURNIP.

HOBO HANK KRUSTY'S KIDDIE SHOW RIVAL

One of Krusty's fiercest competitors, Hobo Hank begins each TV show by welcoming kids to his magic hobo jungle, which he calls Hobohemia. The audience sits on miniature boxcars wearing engineer caps and, at the end of every show, one lucky kid gets to come up on stage and pull something special out of Hobo Hank's Magic Bindle. Hobo Hank has recorded several albums with the Boxcar Boys and his merchandizing tie-ins include toy bindle sticks and bedrolls, a chain of thrift stores, and his own personal cologne, Eau de Bo.

- **Quote:** "All you breezers, boes, and Boxcar Willies, now's the time to hit the sillies!"

- **Hair:** Scraggly.
- **Teeth:** Snaggly.
- **Dress:** Tattered and torn.
- **Demeanor:** Gruff, good-natured, and grasping.
- **TV show name:** Hobo Hank's Hijinks Hour.
- **Show theme song:** "Big Rock Candy Mountain."
- **Sidekicks:** Barrel House Bob, Big Ole Li'l Pup, Klickety Klack, and Switchyard Sam.
- **Charitable endeavors:** Host of the "Bindles to Biafra Telethon."
- **Special Skills:** Plays harmonica; conjures a savory stew from kitchen scraps, tin cans, and cigar butts; and can balance a checkbook on the tip of his nose.

AS FAR AS I'M CONCERNED, HOBO HANK'S JUST ANOTHER SHMOE FROM KOKOMO.

(Advertisement)

WOW!

BOYS AND GIRLS...

IF YOU HAVE AMBITIONS TO BE THE **LIFE OF THE PARTY...** IF YOU WANT TO **BE POPULAR** AND **IN DEMAND** AT SOCIAL GATHERINGS...THIS AD PROBABLY LOOKS LIKE THE **OPPORTUNITY** YOU'VE BEEN WAITING FOR!

KRUSTY'S KNEE-SLAPPING COLLEGE OF SIDE-SPLITTING KNOWLEDGE HOME STUDY COURSE™

TRAIN AT HOME IN YOUR SPARE TIME FOR THE GLAMOROUS AND REWARDING LIFESTYLE OF A LOVABLE, SOUGHT-AFTER, CROWD-PLEASING JOKESTER!

HEY, HEY, KIDS! WHETHER YOU'RE LOOKING TO BECOME A BELOVED ENTERTAINER LIKE **ME**, OR YOU'RE JUST FED UP WITH BEING IGNORED, **KRUSTY'S KNEE-SLAPPING COLLEGE OF SIDE-SPLITTING KNOWLEDGE HOME STUDY COURSE**™ COULD BE JUST THE TICKET FOR GETTING THE ATTENTION YOU CRAVE!

THIS EXCITING COURSE SHOWS YOU HOW TO TAKE ANY JOKE AND **KRUSTIFY®** IT! THAT'S RIGHT! WE TEACH YOU HOW TO TAKE A PUNY, MIRTHLESS JOKE AND PUT IT ACROSS WITH MAXIMUM **KRUSTIFICATION™**!

KNOW YOUR KRUSTORY
with your host, Bart Simpson, Doctor of Krustology!

MUSIC. IS THERE ANYTHING MORE SOUNDY? KRUSTY, MY PERSONAL HERO AND JOKESTER OF ALL TRADES, HAS LAID DOWN MANY A TRACK. SINCE MOST OF HIS ALBUMS ARE ONLY AVAILABLE IN THE PHILIPPINES, A LOT OF PEOPLE JUST DON'T KNOW ABOUT THE MUSICAL MASTERPIECES OF HERSCHEL KRUSTOFSKI...*BUT YOU WILL!* OPEN YOUR EARS AND DELID YOUR EYES, MAN! HERE ARE...

THE LOST ALBUMS OF KRUSTY THE CLOWN!

DARK SIDE OF THE MOONPIE
Attempting to cash in on the height of the progressive art rock wave, this hastily recorded, ill-prepared album fully illustrated Krusty's ignorance of the genre. It featured covers of "Puppy Love" and "My Ding-a-ling" among others.

GET BEHIND ME, SIDESHOW
Mel playing a single snare with his hair bone. Krusty alternating between screaming and bouts of coughing. Feedback from a can opener. It shouldn't have worked, but it did. Musical journalist and cultural critic Greil Marcus described it as "garage rock with the garage door down and the engine turned on and idling. It rocks, but don't breathe too deeply."

FACE DOWN ON MOJITO BEACH

Recorded during his "island phase," Krusty tried to capture Jimmy Buffett's audience by recording 15 songs about tropical cocktails. The recording of "Drownin' in the Scorpion Bowl" took three weeks, during which Krusty was hospitalized for alcohol poisoning six times. The album also featured an oddly inappropriate duet with Ben Savage on the song, "There's Always Room for Jell-O Shots (But I've Got No Room for You in My Heart)."

GREETINGS FROM KRUSTYLAND

Inducting one of his heroes into the Rock 'N' Roll Actors Hall of Fame, Krusty said, "When I went into the studio to record 'Greetings from Krustyland,' I wanted to make a record with lyrics like Bob Dylan and a sound like Phil Spector. But most of all, I wanted to sing like Don Johnson. Now everybody knows that nobody sings like Don Johnson." Alas, Krusty found a way to sing worse.

THESE COLORS DON'T RUN

Seeking to capitalize on the jingoistic nationalism of "patriotic pop-country," Krusty released this poorly thought out collection of what he called, "twangy trigger pullers." With songs like "The Red, Right, and Blue," "Two Roys Don't Make A Right (No Gay Marriage)," and "No Shirt, No Shoes, No Pinkos," Krusty tried to capture the "traditional values" listeners, but soon after the albums' release, it was revealed that Krusty enjoys the music of Bette Midler, eats chopped liver, and that he briefly dated Janeane Garofalo. Then, on an interview with Country Music Television, Krusty admitted to not knowing what a fiddle was.

WHEN YIDDISH UPON A STAR: THE KRUSTOFSKI FAMILY HANUKKAH ALBUM

Actually the sixth bestselling Hanukkah album of all time, "When Yiddish Upon a Star" is the only recorded collaboration between Krusty and his father. The album found a second life after the rap group Ammobeltz sampled the song "Rivka Got Run Over by a Reindeer," for their gangland epic, "Throw You Through a Window." The record, now sampled on twelve other rap singles, is a sought after collectible by hip-hop producers and club DJs.

The Krustofski Family Hanukkah Album

KRUST

Krusty shocked critics, fans, and people who thought he was dead when he released this album of stripped down songs featuring just his warbling voice and a kazoo. The record was nominated for two Grammys® (Best UPC Code and Easiest Packaging to Open).

the glorious K.R.U.S.T.Y.

ready to diet

THE GLORIOUS K.R.U.S.T.Y. "READY TO DIET"

Clocking in at 137 minutes, "Ready to Diet" is a gritty, hip-hop chronicle of Krusty's struggles with weight. From "Baby Food–I Can't Get Enough," to "I Swallow Gum, I'm Crazy!" Krusty brings the listener through a dark journey of food issues, peppering the music with the horrifying sound effects of popping corn, frying eggs, and electric carving knives. The standout track is a dark tale from his yearlong Rice Krispies marshmallow square addiction, entitled, "Crackle's Gonna Die Tonight."

Li'L KRUSTY

MAKE FUNNY INTO MONEY...
The secrets of yuk-cess with Krusty the Clown!

Feeling the pinch of our collapsing economy? Want to create opportunities for a side income? Do you like wearing rubber things on your nose? Come learn how to make yuks into bucks with the legendary laffmeister Krusty the Clown! He'll explore a variety of economic comic opportunities that include clownery, buffoonery, and general tomfoolery...all for money!

Krusty will discuss such topics as:*

- How to make an idiot of yourself to win radio contests
- The fine line between insane ranting and street performance
- How to make a splash as a professional dunk tank victim
- Will anyone pay you to wear a rainbow wig at a professional sporting event?
- Mooning for moola
- Public puppetry: entertaining with nothing but a tube sock and chutzpah
- Eating disgusting things for money
- Dumb waiter, smart waiter: quips equal tips
- Wisecrackin' lumberjackin'
- How to win bar bets without getting your keister kicked
- *And much more!*

IF YOU WANT TO MAKE CASH FROM MAKING PEOPLE LAUGH, DON'T MISS THIS EVENT!

*Depending on a variety of personal factors including (but not limited to) mental state, blood pressure, and level of intoxication

JUST ADDED:

Dignity Don't Pay My Bills! A Workshop on How to Sacrifice Self-Esteem for Big Bucks with Sideshow Mel!

1. Entrance (greet guests with the seltzer-spraying doorbell and joy buzzer doorknobs).
2. Five Clown Car Garage.
3. "Hair"port.
4. Keystone Kop–Patrolled Security Towers.
5. "Pay-Per-Porn" Satellite Dish.
6. Personal Synagogue.
7. Penny Arcade (includes video and pinball games: The Fat Lady Sits II, Tilt-a-Whirl to Hell, Bumper Car Blitz, and Funhouse Freakshow).
8. Big Time Screening Room.
9. Krusty's Keepsakes Library.
10. Walk-in Cigar Humidor, with three categories: "Everyday," "Special Occasion," and "Exploding."
11. Krusty's first mime costume.
12. Mr. Teeny's 1957–1990 (stuffed by Krusty's personal taxidermist, Rolo of Ethnic Town).
13. Sideshow Bob in the library with the rope.
14. Photos of Krusty with famous people: Richard M. Nixon, John Wayne, and Groucho Marx.
15. Master Bedroom (a.k.a. The Center Ring).
16. Closet of Many Noses.
17. Flying Trapeze.
18. Vanity Funhouse Mirrors.
19. Living Room (featuring only the finest in velvet paintings and balloon animal furniture).
20. Grotto (just like Hef's!).
21. Guest Bathroom (with Krustyco Seltzer Shower and Bidet Set™ and Krustyco Joking Toilet Seat™.
22. Mr. Teeny's Tiny Quarters.
23. KA-POW! Room.
24. Gym and Day Spa (equipped with exercise clown bike, inflatable dumbbells, and House of Mirrors Changing Room Maze).
25. Private Stand-up Stage.
26. Kitchen (refrigerators stocked exclusively with champagne and Slim-Fast).
27. Cream Pie Assembly Alcove.
28. Seltzer Pump (provides running seltzer to all rooms of the house).
29. (Not Pictured) Money to Burn Room (temporarily closed due to IRS audit).

...Krusty the Clown's Dream House!

HEY KIDS!!! LOOK AT THE FANTASTIC RICHES THAT ARE YOURS FOR ONLY $9.99* WHEN YOU JOIN MY OFFICIAL FAN CLUB...

KRUSTY'S CRAZY COMEDY CULT!

1. YOU GET A REAL CLUBHOUSE!

2. YOU GET THE BUZZING MEMBERSHIP RING OF JOY!

3. YOU GET THE DAZZLING, LIMITED EDITION CLUB BOW TIE!

4. YOU GET YOUR VERY OWN WATER CLOWNS TO AMAZE YOU FOREVER!

5. YOU GET THIS "CERTIFICATE OF BELONGING" TO CERTIFY THAT YOU BELONG!

6. AND YOU GET EVERYTHING PACKED IN THIS GENUINE STEAMER TRUNK!

*PLUS FEES, DUES, AND CHARGES!

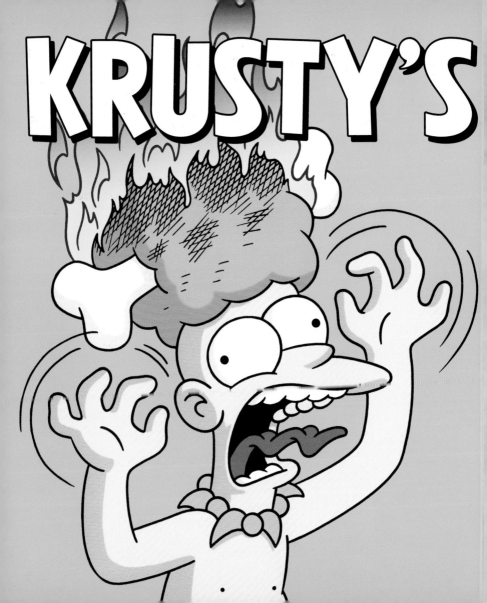

BOTTOM 40

1. No deposit money back on seltzer bottles.
2. Normal-size shoes.
3. Rubber nose condensation.
4. Long cannon fuses.
5. Kids with pablum breath.
6. Gabbo.
7. Mobsters with no sense of humor.
8. Network notes.
9. The way striped pants make my butt look big.
10. Sideshow Bob.
11. Bossy ringmasters.
12. Little pishers.
13. April 15th.
14. Bozo, Bozo, Bozo... (It's all I ever hear!)
15. Monkey funk.
16. Lawsuits.
17. The dim memory of my drunken night with Tina Ballerina.
18. Rodeo clowns.
19. Superfluous nipples.
20. Mishegoss.
21. Handsome Pete. (That guy's rippin' me off! But he is handsome.)
22. Circuses with less than three rings.
23. Uppity straight men.
24. Restraining orders.
25. Rating sweeps periods. (There's only so much T&A you can put into a kiddie show!)
26. The influential Sidekicks and Second Bananas Union.
27. Rancid cream pies.
28. The smell of Sideshow Mel's hair when it's on fire.
29. Community service.
30. The fact that I never appeared on "Circus of the Stars." (Circus? Star? Hello?!)
31. Coffee other than Irish.
32. Bootleg Krusty merchandise.
33. Unicycle helmet laws.
34. Those hurtful mime jokes.
35. Kid parties that start before 3 P.M. (Oy!)
36. Angioplasties.
37. Corporal Punishment's feminine side.
38. The Insane Clown Posse. (Clown Rock in general. It's just wrong!)
39. Raymond J. Johnson always wanting to hang out.
40. The overpaid hack who ghostwrote this list for me.